Friends, Big and Small

Teacher's Guide

Read Well 1 • Unit 21

L I

L says /llll/.
Continuous Sound
(not /ulll/)
Voiced

Critical Foundations in Primary Reading

Marilyn Sprick, Lisa Howard, Ann Fidanque, Shelley V. Jones

Copyright 2007 (Second Edition) Sopris West Educational Services. All rights reserved.

ISBN 13-digit: 978-1-59318-444-5   ISBN 10-digit: 1-59318-444-1   131932/2-13

11 12 13 14 15 RRDHRBVA 17 16 15 14 13

Table of Contents
Unit 21
Friends, Big and Small

How to Teach the Lessons (*continued*)

End of the Unit

I	Mm	Ss	Ee	ee	Mm
I Voiced (Word) **Unit A**	/mmm/ **Monkey** Continuous Voiced **Unit B**	/sss/ **Snake** Continuous Unvoiced **Unit 1**	/eee/ **Emu** Continuous Voiced (Long) **Unit 2**	/eeee/ **Bee** Continuous Voiced (Long) **Unit 2**	/mmm/ **Monkey** Continuous Voiced **Unit 3**
Aa	Dd	th	Nn	Tt	Ww
/aaa/ **Ant** Continuous Voiced (Short) **Unit 4**	/d/ **Dinosaur** Quick Voiced (not duh) **Unit 5**	/ththth/ **the** Continuous Voiced **Unit 6**	/nnn/ **Nest** Continuous Voiced **Unit 7**	/t/ **Turkey** Quick Unvoiced (not tuh) **Unit 8**	/www/ **Wind** Continuous Voiced (woo) **Unit 9**
Ii	Th	Hh	Cc	Rr	ea
/iii/ **Insects** Continuous Voiced (Short) **Unit 10**	/Ththth/ **The** Continuous Voiced **Unit 10**	/h/ **Hippo** Quick Unvoiced (not huh) **Unit 11**	/c/ **Cat** Quick Unvoiced (not cuh) **Unit 12**	/rrr/ **Rabbit** Continuous Voiced **Unit 13**	/eaeaea/ **Eagle** Continuous Voiced (Long) **Unit 13**
Sh/sh	Kk, -ck	oo	ar	Wh/wh	Ee
/shshsh/ **Sheep** Continuous Unvoiced **Unit 14**	/k/ **Kangaroo** Quick Unvoiced (not kuh) **Unit 15**	/oooo/ **Moon** Continuous Voiced (Long) **Unit 16**	/ar/ **Shark** Voiced (R-Controlled) **Unit 17**	/wh/ **Whale** Quick Voiced **Unit 18**	/ĕĕĕ/ **Engine or Ed** Continuous Voiced (Short) **Unit 19**
-y	Ll	Oo	Bb	all	Gg
/-yyy/ **Fly** Continuous Voiced (Long) **Unit 20**	/lll/ **Letter** Continuous Voiced **Unit 21**	/ooo/ **Otter** Continuous Voiced (Short) **Unit 22**	/b/ **Bat** Quick Voiced (not buh) **Unit 23**	/all/ **Ball** Voiced **Unit 23**	/g/ **Gorilla** Quick Voiced (not guh) **Unit 24**
Ff	Uu	er	oo	Yy	Aa
/fff/ **Frog** Continuous Unvoiced **Unit 25**	/uuu/ **Umbrella** Continuous Voiced (Short) **Unit 26**	/er/ **Sister** Voiced (R-Controlled) **Unit 27**	/oo/ **Book** Voiced (Short) **Unit 27**	/y-/ **Yarn** Quick Voiced **Unit 28**	/a/ **Ago** Voiced (Schwa) **Unit 28**
Pp	ay	Vv	Qu/qu	Jj	Xx
/p/ **Pig** Quick Unvoiced (not puh) **Unit 29**	/ay/ **Hay** Voiced **Unit 29**	/vvv/ **Volcano** Continuous Voiced **Unit 30**	/qu/ **Quake** Quick Unvoiced **Unit 31**	/j/ **Jaguar** Quick Voiced (not juh) **Unit 32**	/ksss/ **Fox** Continuous Unvoiced **Unit 33**
or	Zz	a_e	-y	i_e	ou
/or/ **Horn** Voiced (R-Controlled) **Unit 33**	/zzz/ **Zebra** Continuous Voiced **Unit 34**	/a_e/ **Cake** Bossy E Voiced (Long) **Unit 34**	/-y/ **Baby** Voiced **Unit 35**	/i_e/ **Kite** Bossy E Voiced (Long) **Unit 35**	/ou/ **Cloud** Voiced **Unit 36**
ow	Ch/ch	ai	igh	o_e	ir
/ow/ **Cow** Voiced **Unit 36**	/ch/ **Chicken** Quick Unvoiced **Unit 37**	/ai/ **Rain** Voiced (Long) **Unit 37**	/igh/ **Flight** Voiced (Long) **Unit 38**	/o_e/ **Bone** Bossy E Voiced (Long) **Unit 38**	/ir/ **Bird** Voiced (R-Controlled) **Unit 38**

Introduction
Friends, Big and Small

Story Notes

"The Lion and the Ant" carries two messages about friendship. With this adaptation of Aesop's fable about the lion and the mouse, children learn that friends can help one another, no matter how big or small they are. Then, in the final chapters, children learn that friends can keep in touch even from a distance.

Recommended Read Aloud

For reading outside of small group instruction

Yoko's Paper Cranes by Rosemary Wells

Fiction • Narrative

Award-winning author Rosemary Wells tells a gentle story of keeping in touch. After Yoko and her immediate family move to the United States, they write letters back and forth with family members still in Japan. When Yoko's grandmother has a birthday, Yoko sends three paper cranes with a note that she will return one day, just as the cranes do each year.

Read Well Connection

As in *Yoko's Paper Cranes*, the characters in "The Lion and the Ant" learn that distances can be bridged and friendships maintained by writing letters to one another.

NOTE FROM THE AUTHORS

MAKING CONNECTIONS

In the process of learning to read, your children are learning wonderful lessons about friendship, family, and growing up. *Read Well* stories create opportunities for making connections between children's real lives and the stories they are reading.

During whole class instruction, you may wish to talk about relatives who live far away and friends who have moved away. Then you may wish to teach children how to keep in touch through letter writing.

New and Important Objectives
A Research-Based Reading Program
Just Right for Young Children

Oral Language
Phonemic Awareness
Phonics
Fluency
Vocabulary
Comprehension

◆◆ **Oral Language**

★In Units 21–38, language patterns are provided for high-frequency words and for the low-frequency words that are likely to require clarification for many children. For English Language Learners and children with language delays, see page 10 for a list of the new high-frequency patterns.

Phonemic Awareness

Isolating Beginning, Middle, Ending Sounds, Segmenting, Blending, Manipulating, Rhyming, Onset and Rime

Phonics

Letter Sounds, Combinations, and Affixes

★*Ll*

★*sl-*, ★*scr-*, ★*-et*

Review • *Ss, Ee, ee, Mm, Aa, Dd, th, Nn, Tt, Ww, Ii, Th, Hh, Cc, Rr, ea, sh, Sh, Kk, -ck, oo, ar, wh, Wh, e (short), -y (as in "fly")*

· ·

Pattern Words

★*cool,* ★*cricket,* ★*Dear,* ★*dill,* ★*ear,* ★*end,* ★*hill,* ★*lack,* ★*land,* ★*last,* ★*leak,* ★*let,* ★*Let,* ★*Let's,* ★*lick,* ★*list,* ★*man's,* ★*mill,* ★*scar,* ★*scram,* ★*scream,* ★*send,* ★*Seth,* ★*slid,* ★*smell,* ★*still,* ★*swell,* ★*tell,* ★*Tell,* ★*well,* ★*wet,* ★*will*

Review • *am, and, ant, Ant, ants, Ants, Ant's, at, can, can't, card, cards, Cards, creek, crickets, cry, dad, didn't, drank, drink, dry, eat, had, hand, hands, hard, hats, he, He, hear, hen, hills, him, his, in, It, man, Man, me, meet, met, moon, my, near, need, needed, Needed, net, noon, ran, Read, red, rest, rested, sad, Sam, sand, sat, scat, scoot, see, Send, sent, set, Seth's, she, She, shoot, sit, sky, smart, soon, Soon, stand, started, swam, sweets, swim, swoosh, tea, team, tee hee, Tee Hee, ten, tent, thanks, Thanks, that, That, That's, then, Then, think, this, This, three, too, trees, try, We, went, Why, With*

L says /lll/.
Letter in the laundry,
/L/, /l/, /lll/.

Continuous Sound

◆◆ = Oral language patterns   ★ = New in this unit

2

Phonics *(continued)*

Tricky Words

⭐*little,* ⭐*Little,* ⭐*look,* ⭐*Look,* ⭐*one,* ⭐*One,* ⭐*two*

Review • *a, A, are, as, could, couldn't, do, I, into, is, Is, isn't, said, should, the, The, there, There, to, want, wanted, wants, was, wasn't, what, What, where, Where, who, Who*

Comprehension

Comprehension Strategies

Making Connections, Predicting, Identifying, Defining, Explaining, Inferring, Classifying, Responding, Visualizing, Summarizing, Sequencing

Story Elements

Title, Who (Main Characters), Problem, What (Action), Lesson

Story Vocabulary

⭐Dangerous, ⭐Danger, ⭐Rescue, ⭐Postcard

Text Structure

Beginning, Middle, End

Genre

Fiction • Aesop's Fable (Adapted)

Lesson

⭐Friends, whether big or small, can help one another.

Written Response

Sentence Illustration, Sentence Completion, ⭐Sentence Writing, Sentence Comprehension—Multiple Choice, ⭐Summarizing— Story Map, Conventions—Periods, Capitals (Beginning of a Sentence), ⭐Quotation Marks

Fluency

Accuracy, Expression, Phrasing, Rate

Daily Lesson Planning

PACING

Some students will begin the process of learning to read slowly but make rapid progress later. To be at grade level by the end of the year, most first graders need to complete Unit 30 by the end of the 27th week of school. Groups that are working at a slower pace may require more intensive *Read Well* instruction and practice. (See *Getting Started: A Guide to Implementation.*)

> **A BASIC RULE**
> **(Reminder)**
> Make adjustments frequently, moving students as quickly as possible without sacrificing mastery.

ASSESSMENT

Upon completion of this unit, assess each student and proceed to Unit 22 as appropriate.

SAMPLE LESSON PLANS

The sample lesson plans illustrate how materials can be used for students with different learning needs. Each lesson plan is designed to provide daily decoding practice and story reading.

Special Note: If students are entering *Read Well* at Unit 21, begin with the 3-Day Plan to acquaint your students with the format of a *Read Well* unit. If students have been typically following a 2-Day Plan, follow the 3-Day Plan for this unit. You will need additional time to introduce the important skill of story mapping. Story mapping is introduced in Comprehension Work 1b*; therefore, all groups may require a small amount of additional time to guide practice during that activity. (This may mean adding an additional day of instruction for some students.)

3-DAY PLAN		
Day 1	**Day 2**	**Day 3**
• Decoding Practice 1	• Decoding Practice 2	• Decoding Practice 3
• Stories 1 and 2	• Stories 3 and 4	• Stories 5 and 6 and Summary
• Comprehension Work 1b*	• Comprehension Work 3a*	• Comprehension Work 6a*
• Comprehension Work 2*	• Comprehension Work 4*	• Comprehension Work 6b*
• Homework 1, Story 2*	• Homework 2, Story 4*	• Homework 3, Story 6*
		• Homework 4, Storybook Decoding Review*

To avoid excessive seatwork, 3- and 4-Day Plans omit or adjust use of Skill Work. If appropriate, Skill Work 1a, 3b, and 5 can be used anytime during or after this unit as independent work or homework.

4-DAY PLAN			
Day 1	**Day 2**	**Day 3**	**Day 4**
• Decoding Practice 1	• Decoding Practice 2	• Decoding Practice 3	• Decoding Practice 4
• Stories 1 and 2	• Stories 3 and 4	• Stories 5 and 6 and Summary	• Review Stories 2, 4, and 6
• Comprehension Work 1b*	• Comprehension Work 3a*	• Skill Work 3b* (Optional)	• Skill Work 5* (Optional)
• Comprehension Work 2*	• Comprehension Work 4*	• Comprehension Work 6a*	• Comprehension Work 6b*
• Homework 1, Story 2*	• Homework 2, Story 4*	• Homework 3, Story 6*	• Homework 4, Storybook Decoding Review*

---

* From *Read Well* Comprehension and Skill Work (workbook), *Read Well* Homework (blackline masters), or Extra Practice in this book.

6-DAY PLAN • *Pre-Intervention*

Day 1	Day 2	Day 3
• Decoding Practice 1 • Story 1 • Skill Work 1a* (Optional) • Comprehension Work 1b*	• Review Decoding Practice 1 • Story 2 • Comprehension Work 2* • Homework 1, Story 2*	• Decoding Practice 2 • Story 3 • Comprehension Work 3a* • Skill Work 3b* (Optional)
Day 4	**Day 5**	**Day 6**
• Review Decoding Practice 2 • Story 4 • Comprehension Work 4* • Homework 2, Story 4*	• Decoding Practice 3 • Story 5 • Skill Work 5* • Homework 4, Storybook Decoding Review*	• Decoding Practice 4 • Story 6 and Summary • Comprehension Work 6a* • Comprehension Work 6b* • Homework 3, Story 6*

PRE-INTERVENTION AND INTERVENTION

See *Getting Started: A Guide to Implementation* for information on how to achieve mastery at a faster pace with students who require six or more days of instruction.

8-DAY PLAN • *Intervention*

Day 1	Day 2	Day 3	Day 4
• Decoding Practice 1 • Story 1 • Skill Work 1a* (Optional) • Comprehension Work 1b*	• Review Decoding Practice 1 • Story 2 • Comprehension Work 2* • Homework 1, Story 2*	• Decoding Practice 2 • Story 3 • Comprehension Work 3a* • Skill Work 3b* (Optional)	• Review Decoding Practice 2 • Story 4 • Comprehension Work 4* • Homework 2, Story 4*
Day 5	**Day 6**	**Day 7**	**Day 8**
• Decoding Practice 3 • Story 5 • Skill Work 5* • Homework 4, Storybook Decoding Review*	• Decoding Practice 4 • Story 6 and Summary • Comprehension Work 6a* • Comprehension Work 6b* • Homework 3, Story 6*	• Extra Practice 1* • Extra Practice Activity 1*	• Extra Practice 2* • Extra Practice 2 Fluency Passage*

10-DAY PLAN • *Intervention*

Day 1	Day 2	Day 3	Day 4	Day 5
• Decoding Practice 1 • Story 1 • Skill Work 1a* (Optional) • Comprehension Work 1b*	• Review Decoding Practice 1 • Story 2 • Comprehension Work 2* • Homework 1, Story 2*	• Decoding Practice 2 • Story 3 • Comprehension Work 3a* • Skill Work 3b* (Optional)	• Review Decoding Practice 2 • Story 4 • Comprehension Work 4* • Homework 2, Story 4*	• Decoding Practice 3 • Story 5 • Skill Work 5* • Homework 4, Storybook Decoding Review*
Day 6	**Day 7**	**Day 8**	**Day 9**	**Day 10**
• Decoding Practice 4 • Story 6 and Summary • Comprehension Work 6a* • Comprehension Work 6b* • Homework 3, Story 6*	• Extra Practice 1* • Extra Practice Activity 1*	• Extra Practice 2* • Extra Practice 2 Fluency Passage*	• Extra Practice 3* • Extra Practice Activity 3*	• Extra Practice 4* • Extra Practice Activity 4*

Materials and Materials Preparation

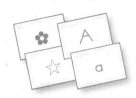
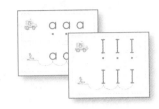

Core Lessons

Teacher Materials

READ WELL MATERIALS

- Unit 21 Teacher's Guide
- Sound and Word Cards for Units 1–21
- Game markers (optional for use with cover-up activities)
- *Assessment Manual* or page 56

SCHOOL SUPPLIES

- Stopwatch or watch with a second hand

Student Materials

READ WELL MATERIALS

- Decoding Book 2 for each student
- Unit 21 Storybook for each student
- Unit 21 Comprehension and Skill Work for each student (My Activity Book 2)
- Unit 21 Certificate of Achievement (blackline master page 57)
- Unit 21 Homework for each student (blackline masters)
  See *Getting Started* for suggested homework routines.

SCHOOL SUPPLIES

- Pencils, colors (optional—markers, crayons, or colored pencils)

Make one copy per student of each blackline master as appropriate for the group.

Note: For new or difficult Comprehension and Skill Work activities, make overhead transparencies from the blackline masters. Use the transparencies to demonstrate and guide practice.

Extra Practice Lessons

Note: Use these lessons only if needed.

Student Materials

READ WELL MATERIALS

- Unit 21 Extra Practice 1 and 2 for each student (blackline master pages 59 and 63)
- Unit 21 Extra Practice Activities 1, 2, 3, and 4 for each student (blackline master pages 60–61 double-sided; 64; 66–67 single-sided; 68 single-sided)

SCHOOL SUPPLIES

- Pencils, colors (markers, crayons, or colored pencils), highlighters, scissors, glue
- White boards or paper

Important Tips

In this section, you will find:

Important Reminders for Teaching Small Groups

Unit 21 is an entry point in the program. If your students are beginning instruction with this unit, you may have missed important tips and features introduced in earlier units. Read this page if you are just beginning *Read Well* instruction with a small group.

★ What's Different?

Starting at Unit 21, Stretch and Shrink in Extra Practice and Smooth and Bumpy Blending are no longer included. Read page 9 to learn how phonemic awareness instruction continues within the context of decoding and spelling instruction and when to use Smooth and Bumpy Blending procedures.

★ Language and Vocabulary Practice— "Rescue" and High-Frequency Words

An additional focus on vocabulary and language skills often benefits English Language Learners and students with language delays. Starting in Unit 21, a vocabulary preview and review is included as well as a list of oral language patterns used with high-frequency words.

Preview the vocabulary word "rescue" before story reading to enhance story comprehension. Review the word "rescue" to increase word knowledge and generalization of use.

Important Reminders for Teaching Small Groups

BEFORE BEGINNING INSTRUCTION
- Read *Getting Started: A Guide to Implementation.*
- Give the *Read Well* Placement Inventory. Do not second-guess where children should begin instruction.

ALLOCATING INSTRUCTIONAL TIME

Instructional time is critical in creating successful programs.

DECODING PRACTICE	STORY READING	COMPREHENSION AND SKILL WORK
Teacher Directed 15 to 20 minutes daily	**Teacher Directed** 15 to 20 minutes daily	**Student Directed as Appropriate** 10 to 15 minutes daily Partner Reading

Through collaboration and careful planning, many schools implement 60 to 90 minutes of small group instruction, five days per week. See *Getting Started* for recommendations.

TEACHING INDEPENDENT WORK SKILLS WITH TEAM

Use the acronym TEAM to teach students how to work independently and productively. (See *Getting Started: A Guide to Implementation.*)

Talk	Teach students how to talk during independent work.
Effort	Teach students how they can demonstrate effort.
Ask	Teach students how they can ask for help when needed.
Movement	Teach students how they can move about during independent work.

TEACHING SMALL GROUP EXPECTATIONS
- Use four or five positively stated rules to teach expectations.
- Have children role play to demonstrate each expectation.
- Have children verify their understanding of expectations.
- Provide positive, descriptive feedback.

TEACHING DAILY DECODING PRACTICE AND STORY READING

Teach explicitly. Use demonstration, guided practice, and independent practice. Teach with fidelity. Lessons provide systematic and continuous review.

Build comprehension and vocabulary with *Read Well's* unique Duet Story format. Concurrently, build accuracy, expression, and fluency through regular readings of Solo Stories.

ASSESSING STUDENT PROGRESS

Teach diagnostically and prescriptively with *Read Well* Oral Reading Fluency Assessments.

⭐ What's Different?

ssstrrreeetch

shrink

Starting at Unit 21, Stretch and Shrink in the Extra Practice and Smooth and Bumpy Blending are no longer included.

STRETCH AND SHRINK

By Unit 21, phonemic awareness activities are embedded within Sounding Out Smoothly and Word Dictation (sound segmentation) in Extra Practice. If children would benefit from additional Stretch and Shrink training (listening for sounds before reading sounds), select three or four words from the Decoding Practice for use in Stretch and Shrink exercises.

SMOOTH AND BUMPY BLENDING

★ 5. SOUNDING OUT SMOOTHLY For each word, have students say any underlined part, sound out the word in one smooth breath, and then read the word.

▲ last ★ slid cool will hill

Smooth Blending can be used as a correction procedure. If a student pauses between sounds, "/s/ • /l/ • /i/ • /d/ or /sl/ • /iiid/ instead of /sssllliiid/," use the instruction procedure below.

- Provide descriptive feedback.
  I heard Bumpy Blending. /sl/•/iiid/

- Demonstrate.
  Listen to me do *Smooth* Blending of the whole word "slid." /sssllliiid/
  Tell me the word. (slid)
  The girl *slid* in the mud.

- Guide.
  Let's do Smooth Blending together. /sssllliiid/
  Tell me the word. (slid)

- Repeat, mixing group and individual turns, independent of your voice.
  Do Smooth Blending by yourselves. (/sssllliiid/)
  Tell me the word. (slid)

- Practice other examples. Return to the difficult word at least three times.

- Acknowledge student efforts.
  You sounded out "slid" smoothly without any help three times!

By Unit 21, Bumpy Blending can also be used to prime students for Sounding Out Smoothly. For example, if students have difficulty sounding out "last," you may wish to have them do Bumpy Blending and then Smooth Blending.

- Have students do Bumpy Blending.
  Do Bumpy Blending of the word. (/l/ • /a/ • /s/ • /t/)

- Have students do Smooth Blending.
  Now do Smooth Blending. (/lllaaassst/)
  Tell me the word. (last)
  I was *last* in line.

> Errors create an opportunity for learning! Provide gentle group corrections. Then, practice to mastery.

9

★Language and Vocabulary Practice "Rescue" and High-Frequency Words

PURPOSE

Additional language lessons can be built around selected vocabulary words *prior* to story reading to increase comprehension during story reading. Continued use of the word *after* story reading will increase word knowledge and understanding across settings. The following lessons may be used to augment a structured oral language program if needed.

PREVIEW "RESCUE" BEFORE READING UNIT 21

In Unit 21, a lion rescues a little ant from drowning, and the little ant rescues the lion from being captured. To prepare children with language delays for the story:

◆◆ FOR ENGLISH LANGUAGE LEARNERS AND CHILDREN WITH LANGUAGE DELAYS

- Collect pictures of rescues.
- Using the pictures, say something like:

  Your new word is "rescue." Tell me your new word. (rescue)

  When someone is *saved* from danger it is called a *rescue.*

  Tell me your new word. (rescue)

  Look at this picture. The firefighters are saving the people in the burning house.

  So we can say, the firefighters are . . . rescuing the people.

- Preview the story. Say something like:

  In your story, a little ant can't swim or get out of the water.

  Is the ant in danger? (Yes)

  The little ant needs to be *saved.*

  Another way to say that is "The little ant needs to be . . . rescued."

  Say that sentence with me. The little ant needs to be rescued.

REVIEW "RESCUE" AFTER READING UNIT 21

Review the vocabulary word after the story using pictures of various rescues.

ORAL LANGUAGE PATTERNS USED WITH NEW HIGH-FREQUENCY WORDS

In addition to the selected vocabulary word for each selection, *Read Well* Decoding Practices include simple sentences for all new high-frequency words. The sentences are repeated below for additional language practice.

ORAL LANGUAGE PATTERNS ★High-Frequency Words Introduced in This Unit
★ When you start a letter, you can start with "*Dear*" someone. What can you start a letter with? *(Dear)*
★ The last thing that happens in a story happens at the . . . *(end).*
★ If you want to [go home] say, "*Let me* [go home]." What do you say? *(Let me* [go home].)
★ A lion is big and an ant is . . . *(little).*
★ *Look* at [my nose].
★ I have *one* [nose]. How many [noses] do I have? *(one)*
★ I have *two* [eyes]. How many [eyes] do I have? *(two)*
★ I *will* [wait for my turn]. What *will* you do? *(I will* [wait for my turn too].)

How to Teach the Lessons

Teach from this section. Each instructional component is outlined in an easy-to-teach format. Special tips are provided to help you nurture student progress.

Decoding Practice 1

- Storybook Introduction
- Story 1, Duet
- Skill Work Activity 1a
- Comprehension Work Activity 1b
- Story 2, Solo
- Comprehension Work Activity 2

Decoding Practice 2

- Story 3, Duet
- Comprehension Work Activity 3a
- Skill Work Activity 3b
- Story 4, Solo
- Comprehension Work Activity 4

Decoding Practice 3

- Story 5, Duet
- Skill Work Activity 5
- Story 6, Solo
- Story Summary
- Comprehension Work Activity 6a
- Comprehension Work Activity 6b

Decoding Practice 4

Review Solo Stories

BUILDING INDEPENDENCE
Next Steps • Principles of Instruction

For Units 21–38, follow the scaffolded principles of instruction below.

Provide demonstration and/or guided practice only with:
- New sounds
- Pattern words with new sounds
- New Tricky Words
- New multisyllabic words

Provide independent practice (practice without your assistance or voice) on:
- New and review pattern words with known sounds
- Review Tricky Words
- Review multisyllabic words

If students make errors, provide appropriate corrections.
- Have students identify any difficult sound and then sound out the word. Provide discrimination practice.
- Reintroduce difficult Tricky Words based on the initial introduction procedures.

If students require your assistance on words with known sounds, evaluate placement and consider a Jell-Well Review.

11

❶ SOUND REVIEW

Use selected Sound Cards from Units 1–20.

❷ NEW SOUND INTRODUCTION

❸ NEW SOUND PRACTICE

> **◆◆ FOR ENGLISH LANGUAGE LEARNERS AND CHILDREN WITH LANGUAGE DELAYS**
> Throughout Decoding Practice and Extra Practice, provide repeated use of the language patterns—both within and outside of lessons. See page 10 for tips.

◆◆ ❹ FOCUS ON VOCABULARY

★ **New vocabulary word: "rescue"**

Introduce the word "rescue" and give examples of its meaning. Say something like:

Your new vocabulary word is "rescue." Tell me your new word. (rescue)

A *rescue* is when someone is saved from danger.

When someone is saved from danger it is called a . . . (rescue).

We could say "The firefighters saved the children" or "The firefighters *rescued* the children."

◆◆ ❺ SOUNDING OUT SMOOTHLY

★ **New blend: /sl-/ as in "slid"**

- For each word, have students say any underlined part, sound out the word, and then read the word. Use the words in sentences as needed.
- Provide repeated practice. Mix group and individual turns, independent of your voice.

◆◆ ❻ ACCURACY AND FLUENCY BUILDING

Repeat practice on each column, building accuracy first and then fluency.

◆◆ ❼ TRICKY WORDS

★ **New Tricky Words: "One," "two," "Little"**

- Tell students the first two words ("One" and "two") don't sound out at all. Explain that they can learn to read those words by remembering how the words are spelled. Say something like:

    Your first new Tricky Word is "One," as in "one shoe," "one pencil," or "one, two, three."

    We spell "one," o-n-e. Spell "one" with me. o-n-e

    Spell "one" three times by yourselves. (o-n-e, o-n-e, o-n-e)

    Now touch the word "One" and read it. (One) I have *one* nose.

- Repeat the process for the word "two."

- For "Little," say something like:

    Look at your next new Tricky Word. The only thing tricky about this word is the e on the end.

    Remember, when a letter has a slash through it, it means the letter doesn't say anything.

    Sound out your new word. (/Lllliiitlll/) Tell me the word. (Little) A lion is big and an ant is *little*.

- Have students read the row. Repeat, mixing group and individual turns, independent of your voice.

❽ DAILY STORY READING

Proceed to the Unit 21 Storybook. See Daily Lesson Planning for pacing suggestions.

❾ COMPREHENSION AND SKILL WORK ACTIVITY I AND/OR ACTIVITY 2

See pages 19–21 and/or 25.

Note: The light scripting in *Read Well* will help you visualize instruction as you prepare for a lesson. Scripting provides an instructional guide and is not intended to be memorized or read to students.

UNIT **21** DECODING PRACTICE I
(For use with Stories I and 2)

I. SOUND REVIEW Use Sound Cards for Units I–20.

2. NEW SOUND INTRODUCTION Have students echo (repeat) the phrases. Do not have students read the poem.

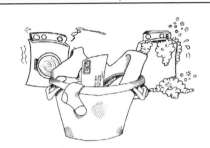

L as in Letter
Capital letter L, small letter l,
L says lll.
Letter in the laundry,
L, l, lll.

3. NEW SOUND PRACTICE Have students read, trace, and say /lll/.

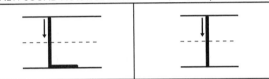

★4. FOCUS ON VOCABULARY Introduce "rescue."
See the Teacher's Guide for detailed instructions.

★5. SOUNDING OUT SMOOTHLY For each word, have students say any underlined part, sound out the word in one smooth breath, and then read the word.

▲ last ★slid cool will hill

6. ACCURACY/FLUENCY BUILDING For each column, have students say the underlined part, then read each word. Next, have students read the column.

✈ try cry creek

● started needed cricket

■ Lĕt sĕt Sĕth

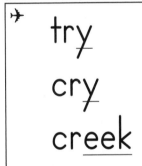

★7. TRICKY WORDS See the Teacher's Guide for how to introduce "One," "two," and "Little." Have students silently figure out each word and read it aloud.

✿ ★One ★two ★Little What

8. DAILY STORY READING

45

Sentence Suggestions: If a sentence is included, use it *after* decoding the individual word.
The sentences may be used to build oral language patterns and vocabulary. Use of sentences
also emphasizes that words have meaning.

❶ INTRODUCING THE STORYBOOK AND THE TITLE PAGE

Identifying—Title

Tell students this storybook is called *Friendships*.
Explain that there are three units in the book.
The first unit is called "Friends, Big and Small."

Predicting

Ask students what they think "Friends, Big and
Small" is going to be about. Tell students the first
chapters of "The Lion and the Ant" are like an old
fable. *Fables* are stories that teach important lessons.
Thousands of years ago a man named Aesop told
fables that are still told today.

❷ INTRODUCING VOCABULARY

Vocabulary—Dangerous, Rescue, Postcard

Dangerous

Put your finger under the first picture.
Something is *dangerous* when it could hurt someone.
What is dangerous in the picture?

Rescue

Put your finger under the next picture.
A *rescue* is when someone is saved from danger.
The cat is being . . . rescued. The firefighter is helping the cat down from the tree.

Postcard

A *postcard* is a card that can be sent to someone.
A postcard usually has a note on it.
One of your stories must be about keeping in touch.

Friends, Big and Small

By Marilyn Sprick
Illustrated by Necdet Yilmaz

Vocabulary Words

dangerous
Something is dangerous when it could hurt someone.

rescue
A rescue is when someone is saved from danger.

postcard
A postcard is a card that can be sent to someone. A postcard usually has a note on it.

6

7

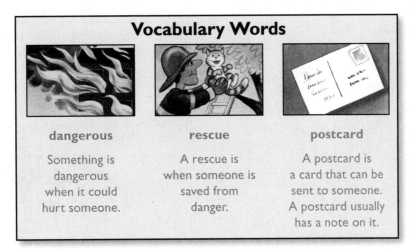

Vocabulary Words

dangerous

Something is dangerous when it could hurt someone.

rescue

A rescue is when someone is saved from danger.

postcard

A postcard is a card that can be sent to someone. A postcard usually has a note on it.

Defining Vocabulary—Dangerous, Rescue, Postcard

DUET STORY READING INSTRUCTIONS

Students read from their own storybooks.
The teacher reads the small text and students read the large text.

PACING

- 3- to 4-Day Plans: Have students do the first reading of Duet Story 1.
  Then proceed to repeated readings of Solo Story 2.
- 6- to 10-Day Plans: Have students do the first *and* second readings as needed.

COMPREHENSION BUILDING:
DISCUSSION QUESTIONS AND TEACHER THINK ALOUDS

- Ask questions and discuss text on the first reading when indicated in the storybook in light gray text.
- ★ • Encourage students to answer questions with complete sentences when appropriate. Following a response, acknowledge the accuracy of the response and then say something like:

  Yes, the story is about the lion and the ant. Start your answer with "The story is about . . ."
  (The story is about the lion and the ant.)

- If students have difficulty with a comprehension question, think aloud with them or reread the portion of the story that answers the question. Then, ask the question again.

PROCEDURES

★ 1. First Reading

Mix group and individual turns on student-read sentences. On individual turns, gently correct any error, and then have the student reread the text.

★ 2. Repeated Readings

Repeat the reading only as needed for comprehension.

DEVELOPING INDEPENDENT READERS

Note the new procedures for reading Duet Stories.

Though the Duet Stories provide an opportunity to build vocabulary, comprehension, and a context for the Solo Stories, the Solo Stories provide children with the greatest opportunity to practice independent and fluent reading. With limited time, move quickly to repeated readings of the next Solo Story.

STORY 1, DUET

The Lion and the Ant

CHAPTER 1

The First Rescue

Who do you think will be rescued?**1** What happens in a rescue?**2**

Little Ant needed a drink. She went

to a creek that was near. As she leaned over the

creek to get a drink, Little Ant slipped, and . . .

slid into the creek.

That sounds dangerous.**3** What do you think might happen?**4**

"I will try to swim," said the ant. She

swam and swam. She swam as hard as

she could. But the little ant quickly grew tired.

What is the little ant's problem?**5**

Soon Little Ant started to cry.

"This is too hard," she said. "I am too tired."

What could happen to the ant?**6**

A kind lion named Seth happened by the creek. He noticed the ant and said to himself, "Poor little ant. She looks like she's in trouble."

With one swoosh, Seth had Little Ant.

He set the ant near him.

How did Seth help the little ant?**7**

8

> **FINGER TRACKING**
> **(Reminder)**
> Continue having children track the large text with their fingers.

❶ **Predicting**

❷ **Using Vocabulary—Rescue, Danger** (In a rescue, someone is saved from danger.)

❸ **Teacher Think Aloud, Using Vocabulary—Dangerous**

❹ **Predicting**

❺ **Identifying—Problem** (Swimming was too hard; the ant thought she would drown.)

❻ **Inferring** (She could drown.)

❼ **Explaining** (He picked the ant up out of the water.)

"Why, thanks!" said Little Ant.

"Thanks! I was sad. I didn't think I

could last. You saved my life. Let me travel with you. Then, someday I can do something to help you!"

The big lion just smiled at the tiny little ant and shook his head.

The lion thinks the ant can't help him. Why not?

9

❶ **Inferring, Explaining** (The lion thinks the ant is too small to help him do anything.)

Note: Questions focus students on important story elements and provide prompts for story discussions. Answers provide guidance, not verbatim responses.

SOUND PAGE

Use work pages from the workbook.

CHECKOUT OPPORTUNITY

While students are working on Comprehension and Skill Work, you may wish to listen to individuals read a Decoding Practice or Solo Story. If the student makes an error, gently correct and have the student reread the column, row, or sentence.

PROCEDURES

For each step, demonstrate and guide practice as needed.

1. Handwriting—Basic Instructions

- Have students identify the capital letter L.
- Have students trace and write the capital letter L—leaving a finger space between each letter. Repeat with the small letter l on the second two rows.
- In each row have students circle their best letter.

2. Drawing Pictures That Begin With /lll/—Basic Instructions

- Have students fill the box with things that begin with /lll/. Students can write the letter l, draw pictures of things that begin with /lll/, cut out and paste on pictures of things that begin with /lll/, or cut out and paste on words that begin with /lll/.

Note: Neat work helps students take pride in their efforts.

★ STORY MAP

Use work pages from the workbook.

PURPOSE

Story mapping helps students organize and write a basic story summary.

PROCEDURES

Story Map—Introductory Instructions

- Using a blank or overhead copy from the blackline master, fill in the blanks as you help students identify the basic story elements—who the story is about (beginning), what happened (middle), and what happened at the end.
- Have students fill in the blanks to create their own story maps of Chapter 1.
- Tell students that a story map helps them retell or summarize the important parts of a story.

Note: You may wish to remind students that a sentence ends with a period.

Writing
Summarizing, Sequencing
Conventions—Period

Explaining—Beginning
Identifying—Who

Explaining—Middle
Identifying—What

Explaining—End
Identifying—What

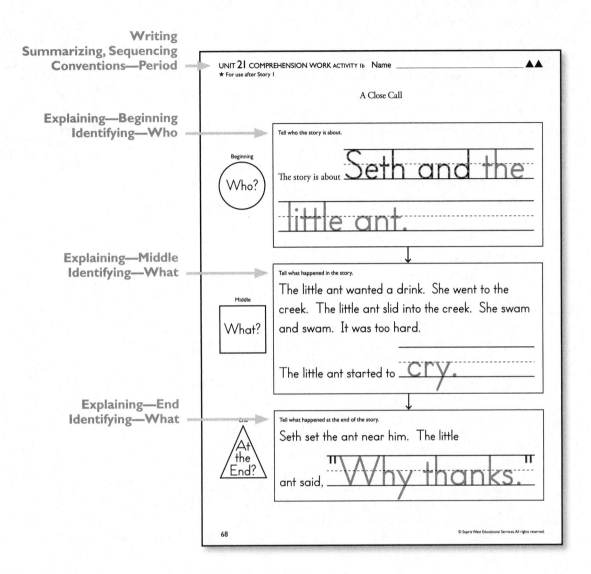

UNIT **21** COMPREHENSION WORK ACTIVITY 1b   Name _____   ▲▲
★ For use after Story 1

A Close Call

Who?   Beginning

Tell who the story is about.

The story is about Seth and the little ant.

What?   Middle

Tell what happened in the story.

The little ant wanted a drink. She went to the creek. The little ant slid into the creek. She swam and swam. It was too hard.

The little ant started to cry.

At the End?   End

Tell what happened at the end of the story.

Seth set the ant near him. The little ant said, "Why thanks."

68

SOLO STORY READING INSTRUCTIONS

Students read from their own storybooks.

COMPREHENSION BUILDING:
DISCUSSION QUESTIONS AND TEACHER THINK ALOUDS

- Ask questions and discuss text on the first reading when indicated in the storybook in light gray text.
- Encourage students to answer questions with complete sentences.
- If students have difficulty with a comprehension question, think aloud with them or reread the portion of the story that answers the question. Then, ask the question again.

PROCEDURES

1. First Reading

Have students choral read the text.

2. Second Reading

- Mix group and individual turns, independent of your voice.
  Have students work toward an accuracy goal of 0–2 errors.
  Quietly keep track of errors made by all students in each group.
- After reading the story, practice any difficult words.
- If the group has not reached the accuracy goal, have the group reread the story, mixing group and individual turns.

3. Repeated Readings
a. Timed Readings

- Once the accuracy goal has been achieved, have individual students read the page while the other children track the text with their fingers and whisper read.

  Time individuals for 30 seconds and encourage each student to work for his or her personal best.

- Count the number of words read correctly in 30 seconds (words read minus errors).

  Multiply by two to determine words read correctly per minute. Record student scores.

Note: If a student is unable to read with close to 100% accuracy, do not time the student. The personal goal should be accuracy. If the student is unable to read with accuracy, evaluate group placement and consider a Jell-Well Review.

b. Partner Reading

During students' daily independent work, have them do Partner Reading.

c. Homework 1

Have students read the story at home. (A reprint of this story is available on a blackline master in *Read Well* Homework.)

STORY 2, SOLO

CHAPTER 2

The Men

This is the second chapter of "The Lion and the Ant."**1**In the last chapter, what was Little Ant's problem?**2**Who rescued the ant?**3**Look at the picture. In this chapter, the lion has a problem. What do you think it might be?**4**

The little ant sat near Seth's ear. "What can I do?" she said.

Seth said, "Let me think. Tell me what there is to see."

Little Ant said, "One little, two little, three little ants. I see three ants!"

Then Little Ant said, "One little, two little, three little crickets. I see and hear three little crickets."

What does Little Ant see and hear?**5**

Seth said, "That's cool. What is that near the hill?"

10

FOCUS ON EXPRESSION

After the first reading and before the second reading, practice paragraphs to develop expression. Select a paragraph. Demonstrate expressive reading, then provide group and/or individual turns. Say something like:

Little Ant is excited about what she sees.

Listen to me read what Little Ant said. "One little, two little, three little ants. I see three ants!"

Now it's your turn. How does Little Ant feel? (Excited) Remember to sound excited.

❶ Identifying—Title

❷ Summarizing, Identifying—Problem (She almost drowned.)

❸ Summarizing, Identifying—Who, Using Vocabulary—Rescue (The lion rescued the ant.)

❹ Predicting

❺ Identifying—What (Ants and crickets)

The little ant said, "One! Two! I see two men!"

Little Ant sounds worried. What do you think is the problem?❶

11

❶ Inferring—Problem

24

STORY COMPREHENSION

Use work pages from the workbook.

CHECKOUT OPPORTUNITY

Listen to your students read individually while others work.

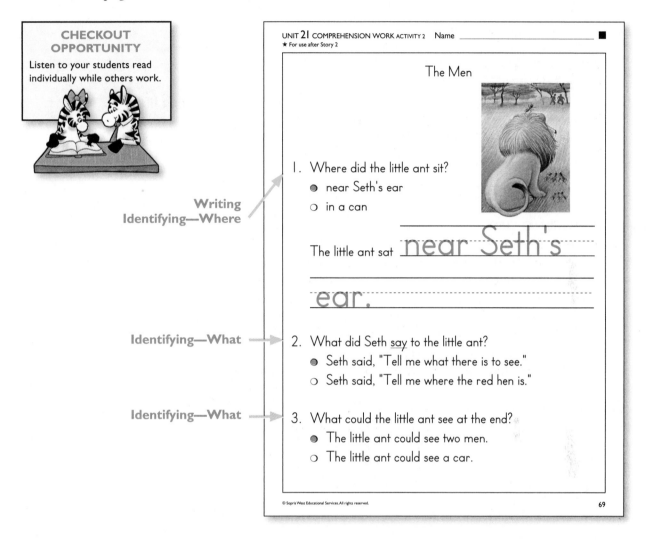

UNIT **21** COMPREHENSION WORK ACTIVITY 2   Name _____ ■
★ For use after Story 2

The Men

Writing
Identifying—Where

1. Where did the little ant sit?
   ● near Seth's ear
   ○ in a can

   The little ant sat near Seth's ear.

Identifying—What

2. What did Seth <u>say</u> to the little ant?
   ● Seth said, "Tell me what there is to see."
   ○ Seth said, "Tell me where the red hen is."

Identifying—What

3. What could the little ant see at the end?
   ● The little ant could see two men.
   ○ The little ant could see a car.

69

PROCEDURES

For each step, demonstrate and guide practice as needed.

Multiple Choice, Sentence Completion—Basic Instructions

- Have students fill in the bubble for the correct answer. Periodically, think aloud with students. Discuss the multiple choice options. As appropriate, ask questions like: "Does the first answer make sense?" "Is that what the book said?" "Is the answer completely correct?"
- Have them write an answer in the blank and place a period at the end.

Note: You may wish to remind students that they can look in their storybooks if they are unsure about the correct answer.

❶ SOUND REVIEW

Use the selected Sound Cards for Units 1–21 or the Sound Review on Decoding Practice 4.

❷ NEW SOUND PRACTICE

◆◆ **❸ FOCUS ON VOCABULARY**

Review vocabulary word: "rescue"

Have students review the word "rescue." Clarify meaning. Say something like:

When someone is saved from danger it is called a . . . *(rescue)*.

Little Ant grew tired of swimming. She didn't think she could . . . (last).

Seth pulled Little Ant out of the creek and saved Little Ant from . . . (danger).

Did Seth rescue Little Ant? (Yes)

How do you know? (Seth saved Little Ant from danger.)

◆◆ **❹ SOUNDING OUT SMOOTHLY**

★ **New blend: /scr-/**

This can be a difficult blend. Demonstrate how to sound it out—moving quickly from the /c/ to the /r/ as though /cr/ were one sound. Say something like:

Listen to me sound out the first three letters /ssscrrr-/. Now you try it.

Once students can sound out "scr," have them sound out and read "scram."

- For each word, have students say the underlined part, sound out the word, and then read the word. Use the words in sentences as needed.
- Provide repeated practice. Mix group and individual turns, independent of your voice.

❺ ACCURACY AND FLUENCY BUILDING

- For each column, have students read each word.
- Have students read the whole column.
- Repeat practice on each column, building accuracy first and then fluency.
- After students read the Airplane Column, ask them which words rhyme. Repeat with the Flower Column.

◆◆ **❻ TRICKY WORDS**

★ **New Tricky Word: "Look"**

- Have students sound out "Look." Then say something like:

  We don't say "I looook at the sky," we say, "I *look* at the sky."

  What's your new word? (Look) Right. *Look* at me.

- Have students read the row. Repeat, mixing group and individual turns, independent of your voice.

❼ DAILY STORY READING

Proceed to the Unit 21 Storybook. See Daily Lesson Planning for pacing suggestions.

❽ COMPREHENSION AND SKILL WORK ACTIVITY 3 AND/OR ACTIVITY 4

See pages 32–33 and/or 37.

◆◆ For ELLs and children with language delays, provide repeated and extended practice with the language patterns. See page 10 for tips.

UNIT **21** DECODING PRACTICE 2
(For use with Stories 3 and 4)

1. SOUND REVIEW Use Sound Cards for Units 1–21 or Sound Review on Decoding Practice 4.

2. NEW SOUND PRACTICE Have students read, trace, and say /lll/.

3. FOCUS ON VOCABULARY Review "rescue." See the Teacher's Guide for detailed instructions.

★4. SOUNDING OUT SMOOTHLY For each word, have students say any underlined part, sound out the word in one smooth breath, and then read the word.

● ĕnd   ★scram   needed   sky

5. ACCURACY/FLUENCY BUILDING For each column, have students read each word. Next, have students read the column.

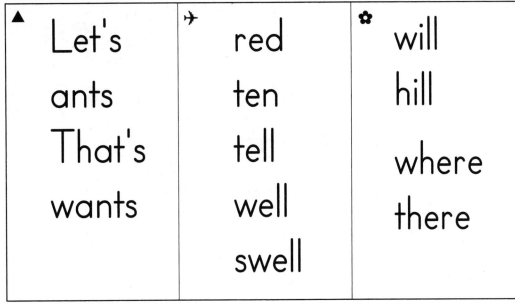

▲	✈	✿
Let's	red	will
ants	ten	hill
That's	tell	where
wants	well	there
	swell	

★6. TRICKY WORDS Introduce "Look" using the Tricky Word procedure. Next, have students silently figure out each word and then read it aloud.

♥ ★Look   two   One   little

7. DAILY STORY READING

46

SHORT VOWEL E

Important!
With this Decoding Practice, we continue fading out use of the diacritical mark over the short vowel e.

WHAT TO DO IF . . .
(Reminder)
If a student misidentifies a sound when reading a word, point to the sound missed on your Decoding Practice. Have everyone identify the correct sound. Have students sound out the word again.

Proceed with the lesson. Return to the difficult word at least three times.

Alternative
You may wish to write any difficult words on a small white board for extra practice. Underline the difficult sound and follow the procedures above.

◆◆ **SENTENCE SUGGESTIONS**

● **end** – The last thing that happens in a story happens at the . . . *(end)*.

● **scram** – The word "scram" means go away.

♥ **Look** – *Look* at [my nose].

Sentence Suggestions: Use the appropriate suggested sentence *after* decoding each individual word.

DUET STORY READING INSTRUCTIONS

Students read from their own storybooks.

The teacher reads the small text and students read the large text.

PACING

- 3- to 4-Day Plans: Have students do the first reading of Duet Story 3.

  Then proceed to repeated readings of Solo Story 4.
- 6- to 10-Day Plans: Have students do the first *and* second readings as needed.

COMPREHENSION BUILDING: DISCUSSION QUESTIONS AND TEACHER THINK ALOUDS

- Ask questions and discuss text on the first reading when indicated in the storybook in light gray text.
- Encourage students to answer questions with complete sentences when appropriate.
- If students have difficulty with a comprehension question, think aloud with them or reread the portion of the story that answers the question. Then, ask the question again.

PROCEDURES

1. First Reading

Mix group and individual turns on student-read sentences. On individual turns, gently correct any error, and then have the student reread the text.

2. Second Reading

Repeat the reading only as needed for comprehension.

CHAPTER 3

The Second Rescue

Look at the picture. Who is going to need a rescue in this chapter?[1,2]

Little Ant said, "Seth, look! Two men! Let's scram."

But before Seth could do anything, he found himself staring at a big net. The lion roared.

Little Ant was scared. She was thinking to herself,

"Is this the end? What will the men do to Seth? One, two, what can I do?"

This is a dangerous situation![3] What do you think might happen to Seth?[4]

12

❶ **Identifying—Who** (Seth the lion)

❷ **Explaining, Using Vocabulary—Rescue**

❸ **Teacher Think Aloud, Using Vocabulary—Dangerous**

❹ **Predicting, Inferring**

Then the smart little ant said, "Ants!

We need ten ants." So she started yelling, "Hurry, hurry, hurry!" Within seconds the ants had arrived. Not one ant, not two ants, not ten ants, but hundreds and thousands of ants.

How do you think the little ants will help Seth?

Suddenly, the men dropped the net and began to run.

13

❶ Inferring, Predicting

STORY 3, DUET

Little Ant could hear one man cry,

"There are ants . . . There are ants in

my . . . There are ants in my pants!"
Why are the men running away? [1]

Seth said, "What? What's happening?"

Little Ant said, "Look, Seth. One

little, two little, three red ants . . . Twenty red
ants! Thirty red ants! Hundreds and hundreds of ants!"

14

> **VISUALIZING,**
> After reading the page, reread the last paragraph. Say something like:
>
> Little Ant said, "Look, Seth. One little, two little, three red ants . . . twenty red ants! Thirty red ants! Hundreds and hundreds of ants!"
>
> How many ants were there? (Hundreds and hundreds)
>
> Close your eyes. Think about hundreds of ants. Why did the men run?

❶ **Inferring, Explaining** (They don't like ants in their pants!)

Then Seth said, "Look at the men!"

The men were running as fast as they could go. Seth and Little Ant started to laugh.

Why did Seth and Little Ant laugh?**1** They learned an important lesson called the moral of the story. What do you think they learned?**2**

15

❶ Inferring, Explaining (They laughed because the big men were running away from the tiny ants.)

❷ Inferring

SENTENCE COMPREHENSION

Use work pages from the workbook.

Illustrating—Who

**Writing
Identifying—What**

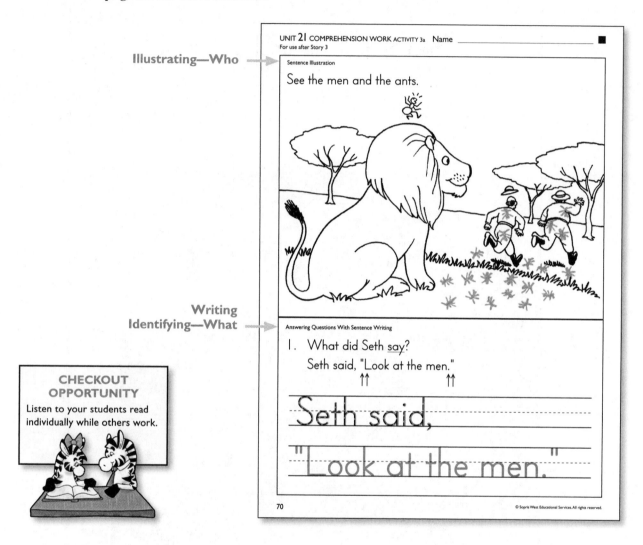

PROCEDURES

For each step, demonstrate and guide practice as needed.

1. Sentence Illustration—Basic Instructions

- Have students read the sentence at the top of the page.
- Have students draw a picture that illustrates the sentence.

2. Answering Questions With Sentence Writing—Basic Instructions

- Have students read the question and answer.
- Have students trace the beginning of the sentence and complete
  the sentence.

Note: You may wish to remind students that a sentence begins with
a capital letter and ends with a period.

★ Also, please note that this sentence is enclosed in quotation marks.
You may wish to say something like:

Seth said the sentence, "Look at the men."
Seth said those exact words so the sentence has quotation marks.
Quotation marks are those little marks at the beginning and end of
the sentence.

RHYMING PATTERNS

Use work pages from the workbook.

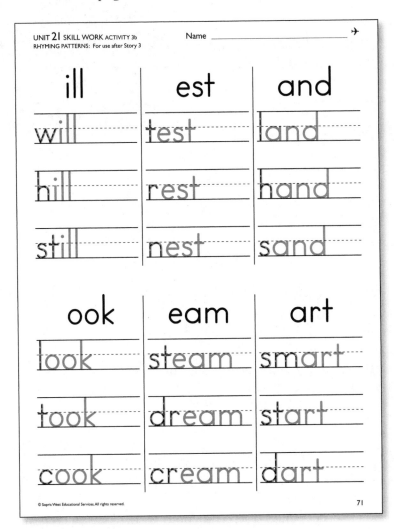

UNIT **21** SKILL WORK ACTIVITY 3b
RHYMING PATTERNS: For use after Story 3

Name _____

ill	est	and
will	test	land
hill	rest	hand
still	nest	sand

ook	eam	art
look	steam	smart
took	dream	start
cook	cream	dart

71

PROCEDURES

Rhyming Patterns—Basic Instructions

- For each box, have students read the pattern at the top and then trace the letters and write the pattern on the lines to make words.
- Remind students to read the pattern words to themselves or to a partner when they finish the exercise.

SOLO STORY READING INSTRUCTIONS

Students read from their own storybooks.

COMPREHENSION BUILDING:
DISCUSSION QUESTIONS AND TEACHER THINK ALOUDS

- Ask questions and discuss text on the first reading when indicated in the storybook in light gray text.
- Encourage students to answer questions with complete sentences.
- If students have difficulty with a comprehension question, think aloud with them or reread the portion of the story that answers the question. Then, ask the question again.

PROCEDURES

1. First Reading

Have students choral read the text.

2. Second Reading

- Mix group and individual turns, independent of your voice. Have students work toward an accuracy goal of 0–2 errors.
  Quietly keep track of errors made by all students in each group.
- After reading the story, practice any difficult words.
- If the group has not reached the accuracy goal, have the group reread the story, mixing group and individual turns.

3. Repeated Readings

a. Timed Readings

- Once the accuracy goal has been achieved, have individual students read the page while the other children track the text with their fingers and whisper read.
  Time individuals for 30 seconds and encourage each student to work for his or her personal best.
- Count the number of words read correctly in 30 seconds (words read minus errors). Multiply by two to determine words read correctly per minute. Record student scores.

b. Partner Reading

During students' daily independent work, have them do Partner Reading.

c. Homework 2

Have students read the story at home. (A reprint of this story is available on a blackline master in *Read Well* Homework.)

STORY 4, SOLO

CHAPTER 4
Tee Hee

Who is this story about?[1] What happened in the first rescue?[2] What happened in the second rescue?[3]

Seth said, "The men ran."

Little Ant said, "Tee hee, tee hee, tee hee. The men couldn't sit!"

Then Seth said, "I can't see the men."

Little Ant said, "The men ran and ran. The men ran into the hills."

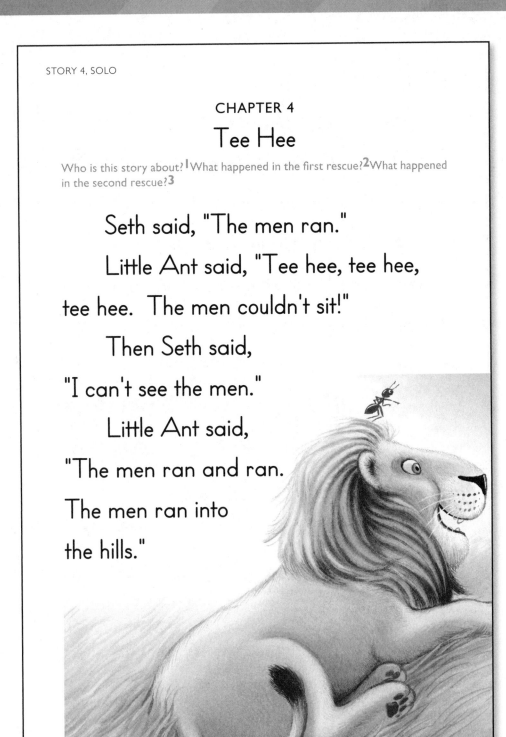

16

❶ Summarizing, Identifying—Who (The story is about Little Ant and Seth the lion.)

❷ Explaining, Using Vocabulary—Rescue (Seth saved Little Ant from the creek.)

❸ Explaining (Little Ant and her friends saved Seth from the men.)

Seth said, "Thanks, Little Ant."

The ant said, "We are smart. We are cool! We are a team."

Seth said, "Little Ant needed me. Then, I needed Little Ant. We are a team."

What did Little Ant and Seth learn?▐

17

❶ **Inferring, Explaining** (Little Ant and Seth learned that friends, whether big or small, can help one another.)

STORY COMPREHENSION

Use work pages from the workbook.

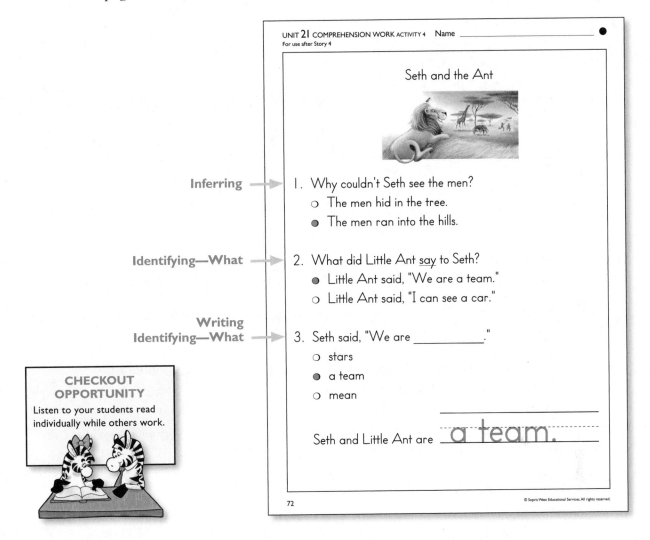

UNIT 21 COMPREHENSION WORK ACTIVITY 4   Name _____
For use after Story 4

Seth and the Ant

Inferring → 1. Why couldn't Seth see the men?
○ The men hid in the tree.
● The men ran into the hills.

Identifying—What → 2. What did Little Ant say to Seth?
● Little Ant said, "We are a team."
○ Little Ant said, "I can see a car."

Writing
Identifying—What → 3. Seth said, "We are _____."
○ stars
● a team
○ mean

Seth and Little Ant are __a team.__

CHECKOUT OPPORTUNITY
Listen to your students read individually while others work.

PROCEDURES

For each step, demonstrate and guide practice as needed.

Multiple Choice, Sentence Completion—Basic Instructions

- Have students fill in the bubble for the correct answer. Periodically, think aloud with students. Discuss the multiple choice options. As appropriate, ask questions like: "Does the first answer make sense?" "Is that what the book said?" "Is the answer completely correct?"
- Have them write an answer in the blank and place a period at the end.

Note: You may wish to remind students that they can look in their storybooks if they are unsure about the correct answer.

1 SOUND REVIEW

Use the selected Sound Cards for Units 1–21 or the Sound Review on Decoding Practice 4.

2 NEW SOUND PRACTICE

◆◆ **3 FOCUS ON VOCABULARY**

Review vocabulary word: "rescue"

Have students review the word "rescue" and use it in a sentence. Say something like:

When someone is saved from danger, what is it called? (A rescue)

What is a rescue? (When someone is saved from danger)

The firefighters saved the children from the burning house.

The firefighters . . . (rescued the children).

The lifeguard saved the girl who couldn't swim.

The lifeguard . . . (rescued the girl).

Seth pulled Little Ant out of the creek. Seth . . . (rescued Little Ant).

◆◆ **4 SOUNDING OUT SMOOTHLY**

- For each word, have students sound out the word and then read the word. Use the words in sentences as needed.
- Provide repeated practice. Mix group and individual turns, independent of your voice.

◆◆ **5 ACCURACY AND FLUENCY BUILDING**

- For each column, have students say any underlined part, then read each word.
- Have students read the whole column.
- Repeat practice on each column, building accuracy first and then fluency.

Note: Use the Airplane Column to build accuracy and fluency on the -ed word ending. Use the words in sentences for students. For example, say something like:

Today, I will rest after school.
Yesterday, I *rested* after school.

Today, I need to eat.
Yesterday, I *needed* to eat.

Note: The Pencil Column provides practice on the -en word family. There are no diacritical marks over the e's.

◆◆ **6 TRICKY WORDS**

Have students read the row. Repeat, mixing group and individual turns, independent of your voice. Use the words in sentences as needed.

7 DAILY STORY READING

Proceed to the Unit 21 Storybook. See Daily Lesson Planning for pacing suggestions.

8 COMPREHENSION AND SKILL WORK ACTIVITY 5 AND/OR ACTIVITY 6

See pages 45 and/or 50–51.

UNIT **21** DECODING PRACTICE 3
(For use with Stories 5 and 6)

1. SOUND REVIEW Use Sound Cards for Units 1–21 or Sound Review on Decoding Practice 4.

2. NEW SOUND PRACTICE Have students read, trace, and say /lll/.

3. FOCUS ON VOCABULARY Review "rescue." See the Teacher's Guide for detailed instructions.

BUILDING MASTERY

Continue working with the skills on each Decoding Practice until students are confident and accurate.

Build fluency (response time) with repeated practice on each row or column.

Give group and individual turns throughout.

4. SOUNDING OUT SMOOTHLY For each word, have students sound out the word in one smooth breath and then read the word.

■ cool   card   Dear   dry

♥ hill   mill   man's   last

5. ACCURACY/FLUENCY BUILDING For each column, have students say any underlined part, then read each word. Next, have students read the column.

✈	✏	✿
rest	Send	wi<u>ll</u>
rested	s<u>en</u>t	sti<u>ll</u>
need	<u>t</u>en<u>t</u>	we<u>ll</u>
needed	th<u>en</u>	smell

SENTENCE SUGGESTIONS

■ **Dear** – If I wrote a letter to [Sally], I might start with "*Dear* [Sally]." If I were writing a letter to [John], I might start with . . . (*Dear* [John]).

♥ **mill** – A *mill* is a place where people grind wheat to make flour.

♥ **man's** – In this story, there were ants in the . . . (*man's* pants).

▲ **Look** – *Look* at [my nose].

6. TRICKY WORDS Have students silently figure out each word and then read it aloud.

▲ Look   who   one   isn't

7. DAILY STORY READING

47

Sentence Suggestions: Use the appropriate suggested sentence *after* decoding each individual word.

DUET STORY READING INSTRUCTIONS

Students read from their own storybooks.
The teacher reads the small text and students read the large text.

PACING

- 3- to 4-Day Plans: Have students do the first reading
  of Duet Story 5.
  Then proceed to repeated readings of Solo Story 6.
- 6- to 10-Day Plans: Have students do the first *and*
  second readings as needed.

COMPREHENSION BUILDING:
DISCUSSION QUESTIONS AND TEACHER THINK ALOUDS

- Ask questions and discuss text on the first reading when indicated in
  the storybook in light gray text.
- Encourage students to answer questions with complete sentences
  when appropriate.
- If students have difficulty with a comprehension question, think aloud
  with them or reread the portion of the story that answers the question.
  Then, ask the question again.

PROCEDURES

1. First Reading

Mix group and individual turns on student-read sentences. On individual
turns, gently correct any error, and then have the student reread the text.

2. Second Reading

Repeat the reading only as needed for comprehension.

**ACKNOWLEDGING
DESIRED
BEHAVIORS**

(Reminder)
Throughout lessons,
make a special effort to
notice the least mature
students when they are
taking steps towards
greater responsibility. Say
something like: [Ellie], you
were tracking every word
that [Jamal] read. It's your
turn to read next.

CHAPTER 5

Keeping in Touch

Seth and Little Ant roamed the grassy plain together. Then one day, Little Ant had to return to her ant hill. Seth still spent his days roaming through the grass, but the two friends promised to keep in touch.

How do you think Seth and Little Ant could keep in touch?❚

Seth's first postcard said:

Dear Ant,
Send me a card.
It isn't hard!

Your friend,

Seth

To: Miss Little Ant
Ant Hill
Africa

18

❶ Inferring

How do you think Little Ant felt when she got Seth's card?**1**
Little Ant wrote back to Seth. She even drew a picture on her card.

Dear Seth,
Read my card.
It isn't hard.
Look at the red ants
in that man's . . . pants!

Your friend,
Little Ant

To: Mr. Seth
Seth's Den
Africa

When Seth read Little Ant's card he roared with laughter.
Why do you think Seth roared with laughter?**2**

19

❶ Inferring
❷ Inferring, Explaining

STORY 5, DUET

Seth wrote right back.

Dear Little Ant,
Tee hee, tee hee.
Let's meet soon.
Let's meet at noon.

Your friend,
Seth

To: Miss Little Ant
Ant Hill
Africa

Little Ant wrote right back.

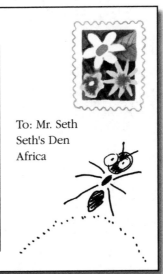

Dear Seth,
That's swell.
I am well.
Let's meet at the mill,
near my hill.

Your friend,
Little Ant

To: Mr. Seth
Seth's Den
Africa

20

FOCUS ON VOCABULARY

Classifying—Place
After reading the page, say something like:

Let's read the last postcard again. Find where Little Ant wanted to meet.

Where did Little Ant want to meet? (At the mill)

Raise your hand if you've been to a mill. A mill is a place most of us haven't visited. A mill is a *place*. What is a mill? (A place)

A mill is a place where people grind wheat into flour.

Soon, Seth met Little Ant near the ant hill. Seth and Little Ant drank tea and had sweets to eat. Seth and Little Ant wrote cards to one another.

What else did they do to keep in touch?**¹**

Little Ant and Seth were happy to see each other. The tiny ant and the big lion laughed and talked—just like old times. They talked about their adventures. They talked about seeing the men run with the ants in their pants. That always made them laugh.

When it was time for Seth to be on his way, the two friends promised to always keep in touch.

I think Little Ant and Seth will be friends forever.**²** What do you think?**³** Why?**⁴**

21

❶ **Identifying—What** (They met for tea. They visited each other.)

❷ **Teacher Think Aloud**

❸ **Responding**

❹ **Inferring, Explaining**

ALPHABET DETECTIVE
Use work pages from the workbook.

CHECKOUT OPPORTUNITY

Listen to your students read individually while others work.

UNIT 21 SKILL WORK ACTIVITY 5
ALPHABET DETECTIVE: For use after Story 5

Name _____

L l   C

L as in Letter

Capital letter L, small letter l,

L says lll.

Letter in the laundry,

L, l, lll.

73

PROCEDURES
For each step, demonstrate and guide practice as needed.

1. Letter Find—Basic Instructions

- Have students look at the first box at the top of the page and follow the directions. Ask:

  What letters will you look for? (The capital letter L and the small letter l)

  What will you do when you find a capital letter L or a small letter l? (Draw a square around it.)

- Have students look at the second box at the top of the page. Ask:

  What other letter will you look for? (The capital letter C.)

  What will you do when you find a capital letter C? (Draw a triangle around it.)

- Tell students to follow the directions in the first box for the whole poem; then follow the directions in the second box for the whole poem.

2. Self-Monitoring—Basic Instructions

Have students systematically check each line after finishing the task.

Alternative: At the beginning of the exercise, tell students the number of l's they will draw a square around and the number of C's they will mark with a triangle. Have students write the numbers on the top of their papers. When students complete the activity, have them count the number of squares and triangles they have drawn. If the numbers are incorrect, they can recheck each line.

3. Coloring—Optional

Have students carefully color the picture, using at least three colors.

Note: If students have difficulty with the multi-step directions, have them do just the first step.

SOLO STORY READING INSTRUCTIONS

Students read from their own storybooks.

COMPREHENSION BUILDING: DISCUSSION QUESTIONS AND TEACHER THINK ALOUDS

- Ask questions and discuss text on the first reading when indicated in the storybook in light gray text.
- Encourage students to answer questions with complete sentences.
- If students have difficulty with a comprehension question, think aloud with them or reread the portion of the story that answers the question. Then, ask the question again.

PROCEDURES

1. First Reading

Have students choral read the text.

2. Second Reading

- Mix group and individual turns, independent of your voice. Have students work toward an accuracy goal of 0–2 errors. Quietly keep track of errors made by all students in each group.
- After reading the story, practice any difficult words.
- If the group has not reached the accuracy goal, have the group reread the story, mixing group and individual turns.

3. Repeated Readings

a. Timed Readings

- Once the accuracy goal has been achieved, have individual students read the page while the other children track the text with their fingers and whisper read.

Time individuals for 30 seconds and encourage each student to work for his or her personal best.

- Count the number of words read correctly in 30 seconds (words read minus errors). Multiply by two to determine words read correctly per minute. Record student scores.

b. Partner Reading

During students' daily independent work, have them do Partner Reading.

c. Homework 3

Have students read the story at home. (A reprint of this story is available on a blackline master in *Read Well* Homework.)

STORY 6, SOLO

CHAPTER 6
Cards, Cards, Cards

After Little Ant went back to her home in the ant hill, Seth and the ant kept in touch.[1]

Seth sent cards to Little Ant and Little Ant sent cards to Seth. Seth sent this card:

Dear Little Ant,
I am well.
I am at the creek.
I had a drink and a swim. It was cool.
—Seth

To: Miss Little Ant
Ant Hill
Africa

What did Seth tell Little Ant?[2] Do you think Little Ant wishes she were at the creek with Seth?[3]

22

❶ **Teacher Think Aloud—Summarizing**

❷ **Identifying—What** (He said he is well. He is at the creek, and he had a drink and a swim.)

❸ **Inferring**

Little Ant's card said:

Dear Seth,

We went to the man's

tent. The man said,

"Ants!" Then he ran

and ran. We had

his sweets. Tee hee.

Let's meet soon.

—Little Ant

To: Mr. Seth
Seth's Den
Africa

What did Little Ant tell Seth?**1** What do you think Seth did when he read Little Ant's card?**2** What do you think Little Ant and Seth will do next?**3**

Little Ant and Seth are a team.

23

1 **Identifying—What** (She wrote that she and some other ants went to the man's tent. She said they ate the man's sweets.)

2 **Inferring, Predicting**

3 **Predicting**

COMPREHENSION BUILDING: ORAL STORY RETELL

- Have students study the pictures, then ask questions and discuss the pictures as indicated in the storybook in light gray text. The circle, square, and triangle provide visual references for the beginning, middle, and end of the story.

STORY SUMMARY

The Lion and the Ant

We're going to retell "The Lion and the Ant."**1**
Who were the main characters?**2**

● At the beginning of the story, what was Little Ant's problem?**3**
Who came to her rescue?**4**

■ In the middle of the story, what was Seth's problem?**5**
Who came to his rescue?**6**

What lesson was learned?**7**

▲ At the end of the story, what were Seth and Little Ant doing?**8**

Let's go back to the beginning and retell the whole story by looking at the pictures. Look at the first picture. This story was about . . .**9**

24

❶ Summarizing, Sequencing

❷ Identifying—Who (The main characters were Seth and Little Ant.)

❸ Explaining—Beginning/Problem (She fell in the creek and couldn't swim.)

❹ Identifying—Who, Using Vocabulary—Rescue (Seth, the lion, came to her rescue.)

❺ Explaining—Middle/Problem (The men wanted to catch Seth in a net and take him away.)

❻ Identifying—Who (Little Ant and her friends came to Seth's rescue.)

❼ Inferring—Lesson (Friends, whether big or small, can help one another.)

❽ Explaining—End (Seth and Little Ant were keeping in touch with one another by writing each other and visiting.)

❾ Summarizing, Sequencing

STORY COMPREHENSION

Use work pages from the workbook.

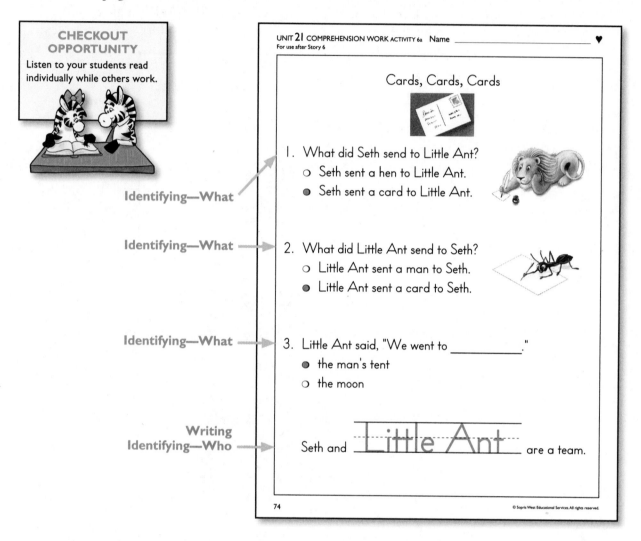

CHECKOUT OPPORTUNITY

Listen to your students read individually while others work.

UNIT **21** COMPREHENSION WORK ACTIVITY 6a Name _____
For use after Story 6

Cards, Cards, Cards

Identifying—What

1. What did Seth send to Little Ant?
   ○ Seth sent a hen to Little Ant.
   ● Seth sent a card to Little Ant.

Identifying—What

2. What did Little Ant send to Seth?
   ○ Little Ant sent a man to Seth.
   ● Little Ant sent a card to Seth.

Identifying—What

3. Little Ant said, "We went to _____."
   ● the man's tent
   ○ the moon

Writing
Identifying—Who

Seth and Little Ant are a team.

74

PROCEDURES

For each step, demonstrate and guide practice as needed.

Multiple Choice, Sentence Completion—Basic Instructions

- Have students fill in the bubble for the correct answer. Periodically, think aloud with students. Discuss the multiple choice options. As appropriate, ask questions like: "Does the first answer make sense?" "Is that what the book said?" "Is the answer completely correct?"
- Have them write an answer in the blank.

Note: You may wish to remind students that they can look in their storybooks if they are unsure about the correct answer.

★ POSTCARDS

Use work pages from the workbook.

PURPOSE

Students practice writing postcards/letters.

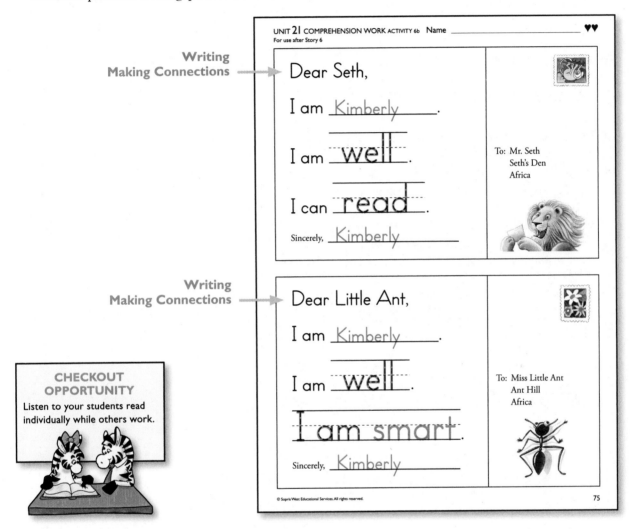

Writing
Making Connections →

UNIT **21** COMPREHENSION WORK ACTIVITY 6b   Name _____ ♥♥
For use after Story 6

Dear Seth,

I am Kimberly_____.

I am _well_.

I can _read_.

Sincerely, Kimberly

To: Mr. Seth
Seth's Den
Africa

Writing
Making Connections →

Dear Little Ant,

I am Kimberly_____.

I am _well_.

I am smart.

Sincerely, Kimberly

To: Miss Little Ant
Ant Hill
Africa

© Sopris West Educational Services. All rights reserved.   75

CHECKOUT OPPORTUNITY
Listen to your students read individually while others work.

PROCEDURES

For each step, demonstrate and guide practice as needed.

Sentence Completion—Basic Instructions

- Have students read the postcards.
- Have students brainstorm possible responses for the blanks and make a list on the board.
- Have students fill in the blanks.

Note: There are multiple uses for Decoding Practice 4.
- Use the Sound Review rows in place of Sound Card Practice.
- Use the whole page at the end of the unit for fluency building and/or to informally assess skills.
- Have students complete the page as a partner review.
- Build spelling dictation lessons from the sounds and words on this page.

❶ SOUND REVIEW

❷ ACCURACY AND FLUENCY BUILDING

❸ TRICKY WORDS

❹ DAILY STORY READING

See Daily Lesson Planning for story suggestions.

BUILDING FLUENT PASSAGE READING

Accuracy must precede rate.

Once students are reading accurately, any type of repeated reading exercise will help them improve their reading rate. Fluency practice should start with easy passages.

1. Set up daily timings on easier passages. The *Read Well* Homework and Extra Practice materials include extra passages for fluency practice. Try to have the students do *four* timings on one passage before they move to the next passage.

2. Teach students to use a tape recorder. During independent work time have students record and then listen to themselves read old Solo Stories. While they listen to themselves read, have the students follow along and mark errors on a transparency. Have the students practice and rerecord a passage when they feel it sounds and feels fluent.

UNIT 21 DECODING PRACTICE 4
(See Daily Lesson Planning for story suggestions.)

1. SOUND REVIEW Demonstrate an appropriate pace. Have students read the sounds in each row.

■	l	oo	Wh	–y	ĕ	t	S	7
❀	a	D	r	h	ar	ac	m	14
♥	n	i	sh	L	k	ea	th	21

2. ACCURACY/FLUENCY BUILDING For each column, have students say any underlined part, then read each word. Next, have students read the column.

✈	✈✈	✈✈✈	❀	❀❀
m<u>ill</u>	h<u>and</u>	n<u>et</u>	scar	l<u>i</u>ck
will	land	set	scat	l<u>ea</u>k
hill	sand	wet	scoot	l<u>ac</u>k
dill	stand	let	scram	l<u>as</u>t
still	and	met	scream	l<u>i</u>st

JAZZY PRACTICE

For variety, provide each child with an overhead and an overhead marker.
In the Airplane Columns, have students underline the rimes ("ill," "and," and "et.")

Practice the rhymes in a jazzy rhythm:

ill . . . ill . . . ill-ill-mill

ill . . . ill . . . ill-ill-will

ill . . . ill . . . ill-ill-hill

ill . . . ill . . . ill-ill-dill

ill . . . ill . . . ill-ill-still

3. TRICKY WORDS Have students silently figure out each word and then read it aloud.

| ☆☆ | Two | wasn't | are | look | A | 5 |
| ☆☆ | what | should | Who | the | one | 10 |

4. DAILY STORY READING

48

End of the Unit

In this section, you will find:

Making Decisions

As you near the end of the unit, you will need to make decisions. Should you administer the Oral Reading Fluency Assessment or should you teach Extra Practice lessons?

Unit 21 Oral Reading Fluency Assessment

The Unit 21 Oral Reading Fluency Assessment is located on page 56 and can also be found in the *Assessment Manual*.

Certificate of Achievement

Celebrate your children's accomplishments.

Extra Practice

Lessons and blackline masters for added decoding practice and independent work are provided for students who need extended practice opportunities.

Making Decisions

ASSESSMENT READINESS

Assess when students are able to easily complete decoding tasks from the beginning of a lesson.

- If you aren't sure whether students are ready for the assessment, give the assessment. Do Extra Practice lessons if needed.
- If students are not ready for the assessment, proceed to Extra Practice lessons. Administer the assessment as soon as students are ready.

GENERAL ASSESSMENT GUIDELINES

- Assess all students.
- Assess each child individually.
- Score student responses on the Student Assessment Record, adhering to the scoring criteria in the *Assessment Manual*. Use a stopwatch to time how long it takes the student to read the oral fluency passage.
- Follow the general instructions at the bottom of each assessment. Record a Strong Pass, a Weak Pass, or a No Pass.

ACCELERATION

- If students read with 100% accuracy and exceed the fluency goal, consider shortening units. Do not skip Unit 22.
- If an individual student reads with greater fluency than others in his or her group, consider regrouping.

ASSESSING UNPRACTICED READING

Do not have children practice the assessments. The goal of reading instruction is to provide children with the skills to read independently.

INTERVENTION OPTIONS—INDIVIDUALS

1. Add informal practice throughout the day.
2. Add practice with repeated readings on Solo Stories.
3. Find ways to provide a double dose of *Read Well* instruction.
   - Have the student work in his or her group *and* a lower group.
   - Have an instructional assistant, older student, or parent volunteer preview or review lessons.
   - Have an instructional assistant provide instruction with Extra Practice lessons.
4. Consider placement in a lower group. If one child's fluency scores are significantly lower than the other children in the group, success will be impossible without additional and intensive practice.

INTERVENTION OPTIONS—GROUP

1. Extend the unit with Extra Practice lessons.
2. Consider a Jell-Well Review before moving forward. (See the *Assessment Manual*.)

CERTIFICATE OF ACHIEVEMENT

When students pass the assessment, celebrate with the Certificate of Achievement. Then, set a personal goal. (See *Getting Started*.)

TRICKY WORD WARM-UP

| one | who | are | wanted | where |

ORAL READING FLUENCY PASSAGE

The Little Tan Kitten

★A little tan kitten went into the den.   8

His dad said, "Sit still. There is a rat."   17

The kitten said, "Look! I see two rats!"   25

The rats said, "We hear two cats."   32

Then the rats ran and hid.   38

ORAL READING FLUENCY	Start timing at the ★ Mark errors. Make a single slash in the text (/) at 60 seconds. Have student complete passage. If the student completes the passage in less than 60 seconds, have the student go back to the ★ and continue reading. Make a double slash (//) in the text at 60 seconds.
WCPM	Determine words correct per minute by subtracting errors from words read in 60 seconds.
STRONG PASS	The student scores no more than 2 errors on the first pass through the passage and reads a minimum of 49 or more words correct per minute. Proceed to Unit 22.
WEAK PASS	The student scores no more than 2 errors on the first pass through the passage and reads 38 to 48 words correct per minute. Proceed to Unit 22 with added fluency practice, or provide Extra Practice lessons in Unit 21, and/or provide a Jell-Well Review.
NO PASS	The student scores 3 or more errors on the first pass through the passage and/or reads 37 or fewer words correct per minute. Provide Extra Practice lessons and retest, and/or provide a Jell-Well Review.

Certificate of Achievement

This certifies that

_____ ,

on this _____ day of _____ , _____ ,

has successfully completed

Read Well Unit 21

Sounds Mastered: s, e, ee, m, a, d, th, n, t, w, i, Th, h, c, r, ea, sh, k, -ck, oo, ar, wh, ĕ, -y (as in "fly"), l

Known Words: By Unit 20, you had learned and practiced 314 words.

New Words Mastered in Unit 21: little, look, one, two, cool, cricket, Dear, dill, end, hill, lack, land, last, leak, let, let's, lick, list, man's, mill, scar, scram, scream, send, Seth, slid, smell, still, swell, tell, well, wet, will

You can now read 347 words—plus many other words made up of the sounds and patterns you've learned.

Note: Personal and Team Goal Setting forms can be copied from Units 16 and 17, or from *Getting Started.*

❶ SOUNDS

Have students say each sound.

❷ WORD DICTATION

Have students count the sounds in each word with their fingers, identify and write each sound, and then read the word. Use the words in sentences as needed.

tan, ran, rats, still

The first word is "tan."
We're going to count the sounds in "tan."
Tell me the first sound. **Hold up one finger.** (/t/)
Repeat with /aaa/ and /nnn/.
How many sounds are in "tan"? (Three)

Tell me the first sound. (/t/) Write it.
Repeat with /aaa/ and /nnn/.
Do Smooth Blending. (/taaannn/) Read the word. (tan)

Repeat with "ran," "rats," and "still."

> **CAUTION**
> Your children may not need Extra Practice. If in doubt, assess students and include Extra Practice only if needed.

⭐ **❸ SENTENCE COMPLETION**

We hear his *dad*.

- Have students read the beginning of the sentence with you.
- Dictate the last word "dad."
- Have students trace the dotted words and complete the sentence with a period.
- Have students read the sentence.

> **DICTATION**
> - Demonstrate and guide practice as needed.
> - Have students check and correct.

❹ ACCURACY AND FLUENCY BUILDING

- For each column, have students say any underlined part, then read each word.
- Have students read the whole column.
- Repeat practice on each column, building accuracy first and then fluency.

❺ TRICKY WORDS

Repeat practice, mixing group and individual turns, independent of your voice.

❻ DAILY STORY READING

Proceed to Extra Practice Activity 1.
- Have students read each sentence from the book.
- Repeat, mixing group and individual turns, independent of your voice.

❼ EXTRA PRACTICE ACTIVITY I—CHECKOUT OPPORTUNITY

Have students fold, color, and read the book.

Name_____

1. SOUNDS Have students say each sound.

I	E	wh	i	L	d	r	a
ar	-y	L	ck	ea	ĕ	l	t

2. WORD DICTATION Have students count the sounds in each word, identify and write each sound, and then read the word: "tan," "ran," "rats," and "still."

1 _____ 2 _____ 3 _____ 4 _____

★3. SENTENCE COMPLETION Have students read the beginning of the sentence. Dictate "dad." Have students trace the words and complete the sentence with a period.

We hear his

4. ACCURACY/FLUENCY BUILDING In each column, have students say any underlined part, then read each word. Next, have students read the column.

♥	♥♥	♥♥♥
hi<u>ll</u>	<u>li</u>st	sky
wi<u>ll</u>	<u>la</u>st	sty
wĕ<u>ll</u>	<u>la</u>nd	steam
swĕ<u>ll</u>	<u>lĕ</u>nd	stream
smĕ<u>ll</u>	<u>lĕ</u>t	scream

5. TRICKY WORDS For each word, have students silently figure out the word, then read it aloud.

littl̶e   one   Who   Look   two

6. DAILY STORY READING

Seth and Little Ant Swim

With one swoosh, Seth 4

sat Little Ant near his ear. 10

Little Ant said, "Look at 15

me swim with Seth." 19

When Seth needed a 23

rest, he sat Little Ant in the 30

sand. "That was cool! 34

Thanks, Seth! Thanks!" 37

3

2

Seth and Little Ant sat 5

near the creek. Little Ant 10

had sweets and Seth 14

drank tea. 16

Soon Seth slid into the 21

creek and said, "Let's swim." 26

Little Ant said, "I can't 31

swim. It is too hard." 36

Seth said, "We will 4

swim as a team!" 8

1

❶ SOUNDS
Have students say each sound.

❷ WORD DICTATION
Have students count the sounds in each word with their fingers, identify and write each sound, and then read the word.
Use the words in sentences as needed.

HAVE STUDENTS CHECK AND CORRECT.

den, then, went, hid

The first word is "den."
We're going to count the sounds in "den."
Tell me the first sound. **Hold up one finger.** (/d/)
Repeat with /ĕĕĕ/ and /nnn/.
How many sounds are in "den"? (Three)

Tell me the first sound. (/d/) Write it.
Repeat with /ĕĕĕ/ and /nnn/.
Do Smooth Blending. (/dĕĕĕnnn/) Read the word. (den)

Repeat with "then," "went," and "hid."

★ ❸ SENTENCE COMPLETION
We sat in the *den*.

- Have students read the beginning of the sentence with you.
- Dictate the last word "den."
- Have students trace the dotted words and complete the sentence with a period.
- Have students read the sentence.

❹ ACCURACY AND FLUENCY BUILDING
- For each column, have students say any underlined part, then read each word.
- Have students read the whole column.
- Repeat practice on each column, building accuracy first and then fluency.

❺ TRICKY WORDS
Repeat practice, mixing group and individual turns, independent of your voice.

❻ DAILY STORY READING
Proceed to Extra Practice 2 Fluency Passage.
- Have students read each sentence.
- Repeat, mixing group and individual turns, independent of your voice.

❼ EXTRA PRACTICE 2 FLUENCY PASSAGE—CHECKOUT OPPORTUNITY
As you listen to individuals read the story, have students color the picture.

1. SOUNDS Have students say each sound.

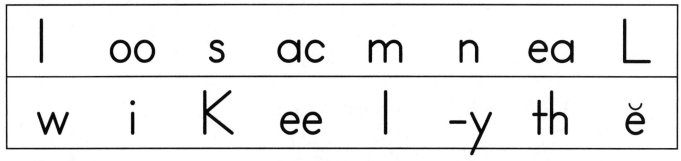

| l | oo | s | ac | m | n | ea | L |
| w | i | K | ee | l | -y | th | ĕ |

2. WORD DICTATION Have students count the sounds in each word, identify and write each sound, and then read the word: "den," "then," "went," and "hid."

1 _____   2 _____   3 _____   4 _____

★3. SENTENCE COMPLETION Have students read the beginning of the sentence. Dictate "den." Have students trace the words and complete the sentence with a period.

We sat in the

4. ACCURACY/FLUENCY BUILDING In each column, have students say any underlined part, then read each word. Next, have students read the column.

♥	♥♥	♥♥♥
tĕn	lid	scar
mĕn	lick	scat
thĕn	lack	scoot
whĕn	last	scram
kittĕn	list	scream

5. TRICKY WORDS For each word, have students silently figure out the word, then read it aloud.

| into | There | a | look | Little |

6. DAILY STORY READING

Name_____

FLUENCY PASSAGE

Ask Me

Will one little kitten start to cry?	7
Will two little hens look at the sky?	15
Will three little ants try to sit still?	23
Will that little cricket land near the hill?	31

Have students read the sentences. Time individual students for 30 seconds; mark errors. To determine words correct per minute (wcpm), count words read in 30 seconds, subtract errors, multiply times two, and record on the chart. If student completes the passage in less than 30 seconds, have him or her return to the top and continue reading. (Repeated readings may be completed with older students, assistants, or parents.)

My goal is to read with 0—2 errors. This is what I did:

Reading	1st	2nd	3rd	4th
Errors				
Words/ 30 seconds				
wcpm				

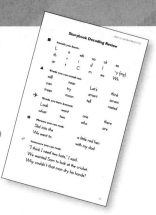

1 STORYBOOK DECODING REVIEW

For each row, mix group and individual turns, independent of your voice.

2 SOLO STORY REVIEW—UNITS 18 AND 19

- Guide student reading, gradually increasing rate.
- Mix group and individual turns on the stories, independent of your voice.
- Repeat practice. While one student reads, have others track the text with their fingers and whisper read.

3 EXTRA PRACTICE ACTIVITY 3—CHECKOUT OPPORTUNITY

- Have students cut out the Letter Cards and arrange them on the top row of the Letter Card Grid to create the words "will," "well," "tell," "lack," "lick," "let," "wet," "then," "when," and "whack."
- Have students arrange and glue the letters in the remaining rows to create "will, "let," and "then."

Challenge Activity: With the remaining letters, have students make a word in the blank row.

1 DECODING PRACTICE 4 REVIEW

For each row, mix group and individual turns, independent of your voice.

2 SOLO STORY REVIEW—UNITS 20 AND 21

- Guide student reading, gradually increasing rate and emphasizing expression.
- Mix group and individual turns on the stories, independent of your voice.
- Repeat practice. While one student reads, have others track the text with their fingers and whisper read.

3 EXTRA PRACTICE ACTIVITY 4—CHECKOUT OPPORTUNITY

- Have students cut out the Memory Cards. While students are cutting out their cards, listen to individuals read a Solo Story.
- Once the cards have been cut out, have the group or pairs of students play Memory.
  Using one set of cards, spread the cards out in rows with the words facing down.
  Have students take turns. Each time a card is turned over, have the group or pair identify the word.
  If the words match, have students set the pair off to the side.
  If the words do not match, have students turn the cards back over and try again.

i	a	e
e	l	ll
w	t	th
n	ck	wh

Name_____

w	i	
	e	t
th		n

Look	little	kitten
Look	little	kitten
at	There	the
at	There	the
A	is	is

Note: Memory Cards can also be used to create sentences. Also, please note that there is no match for the word "A."

I I Voiced (Word) **Unit A**	**Mm** /mmm/ **Monkey** Continuous Voiced **Unit B**	**Ss** /sss/ **Snake** Continuous Unvoiced **Unit 1**	**Ee** /eee/ **Emu** Continuous Voiced (Long) **Unit 2**	**ee** /eeee/ **Bee** Continuous Voiced (Long) **Unit 2**	**Mm** /mmm/ **Monkey** Continuous Voiced **Unit 3**
Aa /aaa/ **Ant** Continuous Voiced (Short) **Unit 4**	**Dd** /d/ **Dinosaur** Quick Voiced (not duh) **Unit 5**	**th** /ththth/ **the** Continuous Voiced **Unit 6**	**Nn** /nnn/ **Nest** Continuous Voiced **Unit 7**	**Tt** /t/ **Turkey** Quick Unvoiced (not tuh) **Unit 8**	**Ww** /www/ **Wind** Continuous Voiced (woo) **Unit 9**
Ii /iii/ **Insects** Continuous Voiced (Short) **Unit 10**	**Th** /Ththth/ **The** Continuous Voiced **Unit 10**	**Hh** /h/ **Hippo** Quick Unvoiced (not huh) **Unit 11**	**Cc** /c/ **Cat** Quick Unvoiced (not cuh) **Unit 12**	**Rr** /rrr/ **Rabbit** Continuous Voiced **Unit 13**	**ea** /eaeaea/ **Eagle** Continuous Voiced (Long) **Unit 13**
Sh/sh /shshsh/ **Sheep** Continuous Unvoiced **Unit 14**	**Kk, -ck** /k/ **Kangaroo** Quick Unvoiced (not kuh) **Unit 15**	**oo** /oooo/ **Moon** Continuous Voiced (Long) **Unit 16**	**ar** /ar/ **Shark** Voiced (R-Controlled) **Unit 17**	**Wh/wh** /wh/ **Whale** Quick Voiced **Unit 18**	**Ee** /ĕĕĕ/ **Engine or Ed** Continuous Voiced (Short) **Unit 19**
-y /-yyy/ **Fly** Continuous Voiced (Long) **Unit 20**	**Ll** /lll/ **Letter** Continuous Voiced **Unit 21**	**Oo** /ooo/ **Otter** Continuous Voiced (Short) **Unit 22**	**Bb** /b/ **Bat** Quick Voiced (not buh) **Unit 23**	**all** /all/ **Ball** Voiced **Unit 23**	**Gg** /g/ **Gorilla** Quick Voiced (not guh) **Unit 24**
Ff /fff/ **Frog** Continuous Unvoiced **Unit 25**	**Uu** /uuu/ **Umbrella** Continuous Voiced (Short) **Unit 26**	**er** /er/ **Sister** Voiced (R-Controlled) **Unit 27**	**oo** /oo/ **Book** Voiced (Short) **Unit 27**	**Yy** /y-/ **Yarn** Quick Voiced **Unit 28**	**Aa** /a/ **Ago** Voiced (Schwa) **Unit 28**
Pp /p/ **Pig** Quick Unvoiced (not puh) **Unit 29**	**ay** /ay/ **Hay** Voiced **Unit 29**	**Vv** /vvv/ **Volcano** Continuous Voiced **Unit 30**	**Qu/qu** /qu/ **Quake** Quick Unvoiced **Unit 31**	**Jj** /j/ **Jaguar** Quick Voiced (not juh) **Unit 32**	**Xx** /ksss/ **Fox** Continuous Unvoiced **Unit 33**
or /or/ **Horn** Voiced (R-Controlled) **Unit 33**	**Zz** /zzz/ **Zebra** Continuous Voiced **Unit 34**	**a_e** /a_e/ **Cake** Bossy E Voiced (Long) **Unit 34**	**-y** /-y/ **Baby** Voiced **Unit 35**	**i_e** /i_e/ **Kite** Bossy E Voiced (Long) **Unit 35**	**ou** /ou/ **Cloud** Voiced **Unit 36**
ow /ow/ **Cow** Voiced **Unit 36**	**Ch/ch** /ch/ **Chicken** Quick Unvoiced **Unit 37**	**ai** /ai/ **Rain** Voiced (Long) **Unit 37**	**igh** /igh/ **Flight** Voiced (Long) **Unit 38**	**o_e** /o_e/ **Bone** Bossy E Voiced (Long) **Unit 38**	**ir** /ir/ **Bird** Voiced (R-Controlled) **Unit 38**

Introduction
Sweet Otter Friends

Story Notes

Birthday celebrations are both exciting and a little anxiety producing for young children. Join Otto Otter as he relaxes and enjoys his first birthday party with a scavenger hunt. The children will have fun following the antics of Otto and his friends as they follow written clues to the big birthday treat.

Recommended Read Aloud

For reading outside of small group instruction

Toot & Puddle by Holly Hobbie

Fiction

Toot & Puddle captures the imagination of young and old with cheerful postcards from one friend to another. As Toot travels, he sends news from around the world to his homebody friend, Puddle. At the story's end, the pigs reunite and celebrate their friendship and their differences. The children's enthusiasm for letter writing will grow as each treasured postcard is read.

Read Well Connection

The *Read Well* stories in Units 21 and 22 are written around a theme of written communication. Just as the children look forward to each postcard in *Toot & Puddle*, Otto and his friends look forward to the written clues in their scavenger hunt.

NOTE FROM THE AUTHORS

> **TARGETED PRACTICE MAKES PERFECT**
>
> Confidence comes from high rates of success. With each succeeding unit, children are mastering the basics of reading. To maintain confidence, keep practice focused on passages composed of the sounds learned.

New and Important Objectives
A Research-Based Reading Program
Just Right for Young Children

Oral Language
Phonemic Awareness
Phonics
Fluency
Vocabulary
Comprehension

◆◆ Oral Language

In Units 21–38, language patterns are provided for high-frequency words and for the low-frequency words that are likely to require clarification for many children. For English Language Learners and children with language delays, see page 10 for a list of the new high-frequency patterns.

Phonemic Awareness

Isolating Beginning, Middle, Ending Sounds, Segmenting, Blending, Manipulating, Rhyming, Onset and Rime

O says /ooo/.
Otter on a log,
/O/, /o/, /ooo/.

Continuous Sound

Phonics

Letter Sounds, Combinations, and Affixes

★Oo, ★cl-, ★tw-, ★-le

Review • Ss, Ee, ee, Mm, Aa, Dd, th, Nn, Tt, Ww, Ii, Th, Hh, Cc, Rr, ea, sh, Sh, Kk, -ck, oo, ar, wh, Wh, e (short), -y (as in "fly"), Ll

Pattern Words

★clam, ★clams, ★clean, ★clock, ★cost, ★cot, ★doodle, ★dot, ★hidden, ★hot, ★lend, ★loss, ★lost, ★lot, ★mom, ★moss, ★moth, ★needle, ★nodded, ★not, ★Not, ★on, ★rattle, ★rock, ★rocks, ★Rod, ★seal, ★seals, ★settle, ★shell, ★shoots, ★slam, ★sleek, ★smooth, ★Tess, ★tot, ★twist

Review • An, and, at, At, can, can't, card, cool, crack, dad, did, didn't, eat, Eat, eats, Eats, hard, hat, he, He, hear, hid, hit, hoot, I, I'm, in, ink, it, It, it's, It's, land, last, let, Let's, *little, man, mat, me, Me, meat, meet, Meet, met, Mom, my, neat, need, Need, needs, noon, read, Read, rest, room, Sam, sand, sea, Seal, Seals, see, See, she, She, shoot, shy, Sid, smack, Smack, smell, snack, Soon, started, still, swam, sweet, swell, swim, swims, swish, swoosh, Tee hee, tell, thanks, Thanks, that, That, That's, them, then, Then, thick, think, Think, this, This, three, too, treat, we, We, well, Well, wet, whack, Whack, wham, whoosh, will, with, With

*Note: Occasionally a Tricky Word (e.g., "little") will be gradually moved from the Tricky Word category to the Pattern Word category as a pattern is established.

◆◆ = Oral language patterns ★ = New in this unit

2

Phonics *(continued)*

Tricky Words

⭐*camel,* ⭐*listen,* ⭐*Listen,* ⭐*mammal,* ⭐*mammals,* ⭐*otter,* ⭐*Otter,* ⭐*otters,* ⭐*Otters,* ⭐*Otto,* ⭐*Otto's*

Review • *a, A, are, as, As, could, do, has, hasn't, his, I, into, is, Is, isn't, look, Look, one, said, should, the, The, there, There, to, two, Two, wants, was, wasn't, what, What, where, Where, Who*

Comprehension

Comprehension Strategies

Building Knowledge, Priming Background Knowledge, Making Connections, Predicting, Identifying, Describing, Defining, Applying, Explaining, Inferring, Affirming, Classifying, Responding, Visualizing, Questioning, Summarizing

. . . .

Story Elements

Title, Who (Character), Want (Goal), What (Action)

. . . .

Story Vocabulary

⭐Otter, ⭐Celebration, ⭐Clue

. . . .

Expository Text Elements

Fact, ⭐Topic—Headings

. . . .

Genre

Nonfiction • Expository

Fiction • Narrative With Factual Content

. . . .

Lessons

Facts can help you identify and classify mammals. (First introduced in Unit 11)

Each animal has its own way of adapting to its environment. (First introduced in Unit 13)

⭐Learn how to use clues. They will help you find things.

. . . .

Written Response

Sentence Completion, Sentence Writing, Sentence Comprehension—Multiple Choice, Conventions—Periods, Capitals (Beginning of a Sentence), Quotation Marks

---

Fluency

Accuracy, Expression, Phrasing, Rate

Daily Lesson Planning

PACING

Some students will begin the process of learning to read slowly but make rapid progress later. To be at grade level by the end of the year, most first graders need to complete Unit 30 by the end of the 27th week of school. Groups that are working at a slower pace may require more intensive *Read Well* instruction and practice. (See *Getting Started: A Guide to Implementation*.)

A BASIC RULE
(Reminder)
Make adjustments frequently, moving students as quickly as possible without sacrificing mastery.

ASSESSMENT

Upon completion of this unit, assess each student and proceed to Unit 23 as appropriate.

SAMPLE LESSON PLANS

The sample lesson plans illustrate how materials can be used for students with different learning needs. Each lesson plan is designed to provide daily decoding practice and story reading.

2-DAY PLAN • *Acceleration*

Day 1	**Day 2**
• Decoding Practice 1	• Decoding Practice 2
• Stories 1 and 2 and Fact Summary	• Stories 3 and 5
• Comprehension Work 1b*	• Comprehension Work 3*
• Comprehension Work 2a*	• Comprehension Work 5*
• Homework 1, Story 2*	• Homework 2, Story 4*
	• Homework 3, Story 6*

In this 2-Day Plan, students skip Decoding Practice 3 and Stories 4 and 6. (Stories 4 and 6 are included in the homework schedule.) Do not assign Comprehension Work 6 unless students have read the story.)

Important Note: Introduce the Tricky Word "Listen" before Story 5.

3-DAY PLAN

Day 1	**Day 2**	**Day 3**
• Decoding Practice 1	• Decoding Practice 2	• Decoding Practice 3
• Stories 1 and 2 and Fact Summary	• Stories 3 and 4	• Stories 5 and 6
• Comprehension Work 1b*	• Comprehension Work 3*	• Comprehension Work 5*
• Comprehension Work 2a*	• Skill Work 4*	• Comprehension Work 6*
• Homework 1, Story 2*	• Homework 2, Story 4*	• Homework 3, Story 6*
		• Homework 4, Storybook Decoding Review*

To avoid excessive seat-work, 2-, 3-, and 4-Day Plans omit or adjust use of Skill Work. If appropriate, Skill Work 1a, 2b, and 4 can be used anytime during or after this unit as independent work or homework.

4-DAY PLAN

Day 1	**Day 2**	**Day 3**	**Day 4**
• Decoding Practice 1	• Decoding Practice 2	• Decoding Practice 3	• Decoding Practice 4
• Stories 1 and 2 and Fact Summary	• Stories 3 and 4	• Stories 5 and 6	• Review Stories 2, 4, and 6
• Comprehension Work 1b*	• Comprehension Work 3*	• Comprehension Work 5*	• Comprehension Work 6*
• Comprehension Work 2a*	• Skill Work 4*	• Homework 3, Story 6*	• Homework 4, Storybook Decoding Review*
• Homework 1, Story 2*	• Homework 2, Story 4*		

* From *Read Well* Comprehension and Skill Work (workbook), *Read Well* Homework (blackline masters), or Extra Practice in this book.

6-DAY PLAN • *Pre-Intervention*

Day 1
- Decoding Practice 1
- Story 1
- Skill Work 1a* (Optional)
- Comprehension Work 1b*

Day 2
- Review Decoding Practice 1
- Story 2 and Fact Summary
- Comprehension Work 2a*
- Skill Work 2b* (Optional)
- Homework 1, Story 2*

Day 3
- Decoding Practice 2
- Story 3
- Comprehension Work 3*

Day 4
- Review Decoding Practice 2
- Story 4
- Comprehension Work 4*
- Homework 2, Story 4*

Day 5
- Decoding Practice 3
- Story 5
- Comprehension Work 5*
- Homework 4, Storybook Decoding Review*

Day 6
- Decoding Practice 4
- Story 6
- Comprehension Work 6*
- Homework 3, Story 6*

PRE-INTERVENTION AND INTERVENTION

See *Getting Started: A Guide to Implementation* for information on how to achieve mastery at a faster pace with students who require six or more days of instruction.

8-DAY PLAN • *Intervention*

Day 1
- Decoding Practice 1
- Story 1
- Skill Work 1a* (Optional)
- Comprehension Work 1b*

Day 2
- Review Decoding Practice 1
- Story 2 and Fact Summary
- Comprehension Work 2a*
- Skill Work 2b* (Optional)
- Homework 1, Story 2*

Day 3
- Decoding Practice 2
- Story 3
- Comprehension Work 3*

Day 4
- Review Decoding Practice 2
- Story 4
- Comprehension Work 4*
- Homework 2, Story 4*

Day 5
- Decoding Practice 3
- Story 5
- Comprehension Work 5*
- Homework 4, Storybook Decoding Review*

Day 6
- Decoding Practice 4
- Story 6
- Comprehension Work 6*
- Homework 3, Story 6*

Day 7
- Extra Practice 1*
- Extra Practice Activity 1*

Day 8
- Extra Practice 2*
- Extra Practice 2 Fluency Passage*

10-DAY PLAN • *Intervention*

Day 1
- Decoding Practice 1
- Story 1
- Skill Work 1a* (Optional)
- Comprehension Work 1b*

Day 2
- Review Decoding Practice 1
- Story 2 and Fact Summary
- Comprehension Work 2a*
- Skill Work 2b* (Optional)
- Homework 1, Story 2*

Day 3
- Decoding Practice 2
- Story 3
- Comprehension Work 3*

Day 4
- Review Decoding Practice 2
- Story 4
- Comprehension Work 4*
- Homework 2, Story 4*

Day 5
- Decoding Practice 3
- Story 5
- Comprehension Work 5*
- Homework 4, Storybook Decoding Review*

Day 6
- Decoding Practice 4
- Story 6
- Comprehension Work 6*
- Homework 3, Story 6*

Day 7
- Extra Practice 1*
- Extra Practice Activity 1*

Day 8
- Extra Practice 2*
- Extra Practice 2 Fluency Passage*

Day 9
- Extra Practice 3*
- Extra Practice Activity 3*

Day 10
- Extra Practice 4*
- Extra Practice Activity 4*

Materials and Materials Preparation

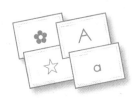 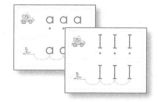  

Core Lessons

Teacher Materials

READ WELL MATERIALS

- Unit 22 Teacher's Guide
- Sound and Word Cards for Units 1–22
- Game markers (optional for use with cover-up activities)
- *Assessment Manual* or page 56

SCHOOL SUPPLIES

- Stopwatch or watch with a second hand

Student Materials

READ WELL MATERIALS

- Decoding Book 2 for each student
- Unit 22 Storybook for each student
- Unit 22 Comprehension and Skill Work for each student (My Activity Book 2)
- Unit 22 Certificate of Achievement (blackline master page 57)
- Unit 22 Homework for each student (blackline masters)
  See *Getting Started* for suggested homework routines.

SCHOOL SUPPLIES

- Pencils, colors (optional—markers, crayons, or colored pencils)

Make one copy per student of each blackline master as appropriate for the group.

Note: For new or difficult Comprehension and Skill Work activities, make overhead transparencies from the blackline masters. Use the transparencies to demonstrate and guide practice.

Extra Practice Lessons

Note: Use these lessons only if needed.

Student Materials

READ WELL MATERIALS

- Unit 22 Extra Practice 1 and 2 for each student (blackline master pages 59 and 63)
- Unit 22 Extra Practice Activities 1, 2, 3, and 4 for each student (blackline master pages 60–61 double-sided; 64 single-sided; 66–67 single-sided; 68 single-sided)

SCHOOL SUPPLIES

- Pencils, colors (markers, crayons, or colored pencils), highlighters, scissors, glue
- White boards or paper

Important Tips

In this section, you will find:

★ **Reading for Information—Using Headings to Identify Subtopics**

With this unit, children begin learning to read for information, using headings to preview and review information learned.

★ **Jell-Well Reviews—Units 21–38**

When children enter school with little or no literacy background, or are among the few children for whom learning to read is very difficult, a periodic review of earlier units is sometimes necessary.

★ **Language and Vocabulary Practice— "Mammal" and High-Frequency Words**

An additional focus on vocabulary and language skills often benefits English Language Learners and students with language delays.

Preview the vocabulary word "mammal" before story reading. Recursive use of the word "mammal" provides students with an opportunity to increase their knowledge of the word, and an opportunity to continue practicing the skill of classifying.

A list of oral language patterns used with high-frequency words is also provided for additional emphasis and practice across settings.

★ Reading for Information
Using Headings to Identify Subtopics

PURPOSE

With this unit, children continue learning to read for information. In previous units, children have had multiple opportunities to identify topics (what a nonfiction passage is about) and to identify facts.

Beginning with Unit 22, students will learn to use headings to preview and review what information will be learned. Instruction is explicit. You will demonstrate and then guide practice across multiple units as children begin learning basic strategies for working with nonfiction text structures.

HEADINGS

After students read the underlined heading "What are otters?" say something like:

The underlined words are called a heading. The words tell you what we will read about next. Read the underlined words again.

(What are otters?)

You are going to learn what otters are.

Demonstration ———▶ What will you learn? (What otters are)

HEADINGS

Before students read, have them find the two headings on this page. Say something like:

Find the first heading on this page.

Read the underlined words.

(Where can we see sea otters?)

What will you learn?

Guided Practice ———▶ (Where we can see sea otters)

Find the next heading. It's in small print, so I'll read it. The heading says "How do otters stay warm?"

Repeated Independent Practice ———▶ What else will we learn about on this page?

(How otters stay warm)

After students read the passage, they will summarize what they have learned and refer back to the headings to verify or affirm information learned.

★Jell-Well Reviews—Units 21–38

PURPOSE

For children who begin learning to read with less literacy preparation and skill, a periodic review is sometimes critical to move forward.

WHEN TO DO A JELL-WELL REVIEW

When a child or group of children receive a Weak Pass for two consecutive units, provide a Jell-Well Review. A Jell-Well Review for a group can often allow more rapid progress through later units.

PROCEDURES

Determine when the individual child or the group last received Strong Passes. Go back to this unit and proceed forward again—as rapidly as possible. Develop daily Jell-Well lessons that include:

- **Sound and Word Card Practice**

  Practice known sounds with a special emphasis on vowels.

- **Accuracy and Fluency Building**

  Have students work daily on the words found in the Accuracy and Fluency columns in Decoding Practice 4. Use the Accuracy columns to build discrimination (lick, lack, look, luck) and the Fluency columns to build speed of recognition (lick, sick, Nick, Rick).

- **Word Practice**

  Have students work in the Decoding Practice. Incorporate dictation, word building, and blending games in your practice. (See *Getting Started: A Guide to Implementation* and examples from the Teacher's Guides.)

- **Daily Solo Story Reading With Repeated Readings**

  Provide daily repeated readings of Solo Stories from the review unit. Homework and Extra Practice provide excellent resources. (Some teachers copy the Homework to create Solo Story notebooks.)

LESSON PLANNER

A Jell-Well Lesson Planner and more detailed information can be found in *Getting Started: A Guide to Implementation* and in the *Assessment Manual*.

⭐ Language and Vocabulary Practice "Mammal" and High-Frequency Words

PURPOSE

Additional language lessons around selected vocabulary words prior to story reading build comprehension. Continued use of the word after story reading will also increase word knowledge and understanding across settings. The following lessons may be used to augment a structured oral language program.

◆◆ **FOR ENGLISH LANGUAGE LEARNERS AND CHILDREN WITH LANGUAGE DELAYS**

PREVIEW "MAMMAL" BEFORE READING UNIT 22

In Unit 22, students expand their knowledge of mammals by learning about sea otters and seals.

- Collect pictures of sea mammals with their babies.
- Using the pictures, say something like:

  Let's see if we can remember the four facts we learned earlier in the year about *mammals*. Mammals have a . . . **Point to the mammal's backbone** . . . (backbone).

  Mammals breathe . . . **Point to the mammal's nose** . . . (air).

  Mammals have hair or . . . **Point to the mammal's fur** . . . (fur).

  Mammals take care of their . . . **Point to the mammal's baby** . . . (babies).

  Animals that have a backbone and hair or fur, breathe air, and take care of their babies are called . . . (*mammals*).

  Does a [seal] have a backbone? (Yes)

  Does a [seal] breathe air? (Yes)

  Does a [seal] have fur? (Yes)

  Does a [seal] take care of its babies? (Yes)

  So, what is a seal? (A mammal)

REVIEW "MAMMAL" AFTER READING UNIT 22

Review the word and classification of mammals using pictures of various animals.

ORAL LANGUAGE PATTERNS USED WITH HIGH-FREQUENCY WORDS

Read Well Decoding Practice includes simple sentences for all new high-frequency words. The language patterns are repeated below for additional practice.

ORAL LANGUAGE PATTERNS ⭐High-Frequency Words Introduced in This Unit
⭐After you wash your hands, they are . . . *clean.*
⭐This is *not* a [pencil]. Is this a [pencil]? (No, this is *not* a [pencil].)
⭐The [book] is *on* the [table]. Where is the [book]? (*On* the [table])

How to Teach the Lessons

Teach from this section. Each instructional component is outlined in an easy-to-teach format. Special tips are provided to help you nurture student progress.

Decoding Practice 1

- Unit Introduction
- Story 1, Duet
- Skill Work Activity 1a
- Comprehension Work Activity 1b
- Story 2, Solo
- Fact Summary
- Comprehension Work Activity 2a
- Skill Work Activity 2b

Decoding Practice 2

- Story 3, Duet
- Comprehension Work Activity 3
- Story 4, Solo
- Skill Work Activity 4

Decoding Practice 3

- Story 5, Duet
- Comprehension Work Activity 5
- Story 6, Solo
- Comprehension Work Activity 6

Decoding Practice 4

Review Solo Stories

BUILDING INDEPENDENCE
Next Steps • Principles of Instruction

For Units 21–38, follow the scaffolded principles of instruction below.

Provide demonstration and/or guided practice only with:
- New sounds
- Pattern words with new sounds
- New Tricky Words
- New multisyllabic words

Provide independent practice (practice without your assistance or voice) on:
- New and review pattern words with known sounds
- Review Tricky Words
- Review multisyllabic words

If students make errors, provide appropriate corrections.
- Have students identify any difficult sound and then sound out the word. Provide discrimination practice.
- Reintroduce difficult Tricky Words based on the initial introduction procedures.

If students require your assistance on words with known sounds, evaluate placement and consider a Jell-Well Review.

11

① SOUND REVIEW

Use selected Sound Cards from Units 1–21.

② NEW SOUND INTRODUCTION

- Before reading the poem, write <u>oo</u> on the board and ask students to tell you the sound.
- Then, erase the second <u>o</u> and say something like:

  Today we are going to learn what *one* letter <u>o</u> often says. Listen to the poem.
- Have students echo the poem for "O as in Otter."
- When you are finished, point to the single letter <u>o</u> on the board and say something like:

  What sound does *one* letter <u>o</u> often make? (/ŏŏŏ/)

◆◆ FOR ENGLISH LANGUAGE LEARNERS AND CHILDREN WITH LANGUAGE DELAYS

Throughout Decoding Practice and Extra Practice, provide repeated use of the language patterns—both within and outside of lessons. See page 10 for tips.

③ NEW SOUND PRACTICE

◆◆ ④ FOCUS ON VOCABULARY

Review vocabulary word: "mammal"

Have students review the word "mammal" and use it in a sentence. Say something like:

Let's see if we can remember the four facts we've learned about *mammals*.

Mammals have a . . . **Point to your backbone** . . . (backbone). Mammals breathe . . . (air).

Mammals have hair or . . . (fur). Mammals take care of their . . . (babies).

Look at the picture. An otter is a . . . *(mammal).*

◆◆ ⑤ SOUNDING OUT SMOOTHLY

- For each word, have students say the underlined part, sound out the word, and then read the word. Use the words in sentences as needed.
- Provide repeated practice. Mix group and individual turns, independent of your voice.

⑥ ACCURACY AND FLUENCY BUILDING

◆◆ ★ New blend: /cl-/

- For each column, have students say any underlined part, then read each word.
- Have students read the whole column.
- Repeat practice on each column, building accuracy first and then fluency.

Note: If students have difficulty with /cl-/ in the Flower Column, write "am" on the chalkboard and have students read "am." Add an <u>l</u> and have students read "lam." Then add a <u>c</u> and have students read "clam." Repeat with "ock-lock-clock," and "ean-lean-clean."

⑦ TRICKY WORDS

★ New Tricky Word: "otters"

The word "otters" will be a pattern word once students learn <u>er</u> (Unit 27). For now, however, say something like: Your new Tricky Word is "otters." Listen to me sound out "otters." /ŏŏŏterzzz/ Later you will learn that <u>er</u> says /er/. Now read the word. (otters)

Have students read the row. Repeat, mixing group and individual turns, independent of your voice.

⑧ DAILY STORY READING

Proceed to the Unit 22 Storybook. See Daily Lesson Planning for pacing suggestions.

⑨ COMPREHENSION AND SKILL WORK ACTIVITY 1 AND/OR ACTIVITY 2

See pages 20–21 and/or 26–27.

UNIT **22** DECODING PRACTICE I
(For use with Stories 1 and 2)

1. SOUND REVIEW Use Sound Cards for Units 1–21.

2. NEW SOUND INTRODUCTION Have the students echo (repeat) the phrases. Do not have students read the poem.

O as in Otter
Capital letter O, small letter o,
O says ooo.
Otter on a log,
O, o, ooo.

3. NEW SOUND PRACTICE Have students read, trace, and say /ooo/.

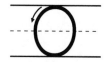

4. FOCUS ON VOCABULARY See the Teacher's Guide for detailed instructions.

★mammal

5. SOUNDING OUT SMOOTHLY For each word, have students say the underlined part, sound out the word in one smooth breath, and then read the word.

▲

on   not   mom   rock

★6. ACCURACY/FLUENCY BUILDING For each column, have students say any underlined part, then read each word. Next, have students read the column.

✈	●	✿	■
smell	will	★clam	crack
smack	well	clock	whack
smooth	shell	clean	snack

★7. TRICKY WORDS Introduce "otters" using the Tricky Word procedure. Next, have students silently figure out each word and then read it aloud.

☆

★otters   Look   one   should

8. DAILY STORY READING

49

Sentence Suggestions: If a sentence is included, use it *after* decoding the individual word. The sentences may be used to build oral language patterns and vocabulary. Use of sentences also emphasizes that words have meaning.

❶ INTRODUCING THE UNIT AND THE TITLE PAGE

Identifying—Title

Tell students this unit is called "Sweet Otter Friends."

Priming Background Knowledge

Ask students if they've ever seen an otter. Ask students what they already know about otters.

Explain that this unit includes a factual passage about otters and a made-up story about a little otter's birthday party.

❷ INTRODUCING VOCABULARY

Vocabulary—Otter, Celebration, Clue

Otter

Put your finger under the first picture.

An *otter* is a mammal that lives mostly in the water.

Making Connections, Applying

Since an otter is a mammal, you already know some facts about it.

What do you know about an otter?

Celebration

Put your finger under the next picture.

A *celebration* is often a party. A birthday party is a birthday celebration.

Clue

A *clue* is something that helps us find something.

In this story, the little otters will follow clues that they find in notes.

Sweet Otter Friends

Illustrated by Ashley Mims

Otters in the Sea
By Marilyn Sprick

Otto's First Birthday Celebration
By Jessica Sprick and Marilyn Sprick

UNIT 22 STORIES

Vocabulary Words

otter
An otter is a mammal that lives mostly in the water.

celebration
A celebration is often a party. A birthday party is a birthday celebration.

clue
A clue is something that helps us find something.

26

27

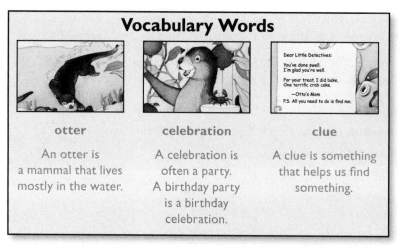

Vocabulary Words

otter
An otter is a mammal that lives mostly in the water.

celebration
A celebration is often a party. A birthday party is a birthday celebration.

clue
A clue is something that helps us find something.

Defining Vocabulary—Otter, Celebration, Clue

DUET STORY READING INSTRUCTIONS
Students read from their own storybooks.
The teacher reads the small text and students read the large text.

PACING
- 2- to 4-Day Plans: Have students do the first reading of Duet Story 1.
  Then proceed to repeated readings of Solo Story 2.
- 6- to 10-Day Plans: Have students do the first *and* second readings as needed.

COMPREHENSION BUILDING:
DISCUSSION QUESTIONS AND TEACHER THINK ALOUDS
- Ask questions and discuss text on the first reading when indicated in the storybook in light gray text.
- Encourage students to answer questions with complete sentences when appropriate. Following a response, acknowledge the accuracy of the response and then say something like:

  Yes, a sea otter's habitat is the sea. Start your answer with "A sea otter's . . ."
  (A sea otter's habitat is the sea.)
- If students have difficulty with a comprehension question, think aloud with them or reread the portion of the story that answers the question. Then, ask the question again.

PROCEDURES
1. Introducing the Story
Before reading the story, say something like:
This story is called "Otters in the Sea."
The chapter is called "Sea Otter Facts."
What will you learn in this chapter? (Facts about otters)
A fact is something that is real.

★ 2. First Reading
Mix group and individual turns on student-read sentences. On individual turns, gently correct any error, and then have the student reread the text.

Note: In this unit, students are introduced to headings in a nonfiction passage. Watch the zebra notes for instructional procedures.

3. Repeated Readings
Repeat the reading only as needed for comprehension.

Otters in the Sea

CHAPTER 1

Sea Otter Facts

Look at the sea otters. See them swim in the sea.

FINGER TRACKING
(Reminder)
Continue having children track the large text with their fingers.

What are otters?

Otters are mammals. Otters have backbones. They breathe air. They take care of their babies, and they have fur or hair.
Tell me five facts about otters.❙

HEADINGS

After students read the underlined heading "What are otters?" say something like:

The underlined words are called a heading. The words tell you what we will read about next. Read the underlined words again. (What are otters?)

You are going to find out what otters are. What will you learn? (What otters are)

28

❶ **Identifying—Facts** (Otters are mammals. They have backbones, breathe air, take care of their babies, and have fur.)

STORY 1, DUET

HEADINGS

Before students read, have them find the two headings on this page. Say something like:

Find the first heading on this page. Read the underlined words. (Where can we see sea otters?)

What will you learn? (Where we can see sea otters)

Find the next heading. It's in small print, so I'll read it. The heading says "How do otters stay warm?" What else will we learn about on this page? (How otters stay warm)

<u>Where can we see sea otters?</u>

Not in the sand. Not on the land.

Otters swim, eat, and rest in the sea.

Otters are sea mammals. A sea otter's habitat is the sea.

What is a sea otter's habitat?[1]

<u>How do otters stay warm?</u>

The sea is very cold, so an otter's fur is made up of millions of hairs.

It is thick and smooth.

Look at the picture. Tell me about an otter's fur.[2]

29

❶ **Explaining, Using Vocabulary—Habitat** (The sea otter's habitat is the sea.)

❷ **Describing** (It is thick and smooth.)

What do otters eat?

Otters eat clams. They also eat fish, crab, and sea urchins. They dive deep into the ocean looking for food. Then they bring their food to the surface and eat it while lying on their backs.

Have you ever tried to eat lying on your back? **1** What happens? **2**

How do otters stay clean?

Otters roll in the water to play, but they also roll for another reason.

Otters are clean. As otters swim in the sea, the water washes off food and keeps the otters clean.

How do otters learn to swim?

A little otter needs its mom. It can't swim well. It eats and swims with its mom. The otter mother cuddles, grooms, and teaches her baby until it is about six months old. Otter mothers take very good care of their babies.

What do otter mothers do? **3**

30

❶ **Making Connections**

❷ **Inferring, Explaining**

❸ **Identifying—What** (They cuddle, groom, and teach their babies.)

SOUND PAGE

Use work pages from the workbook.

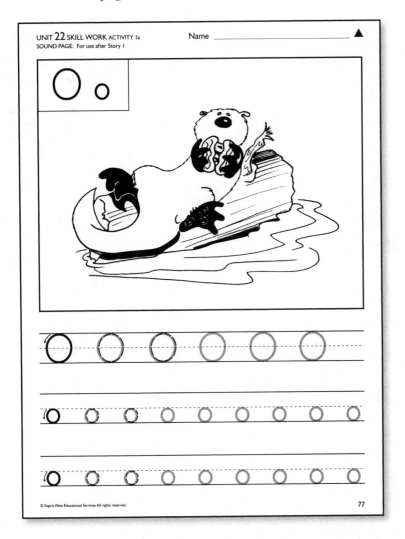

UNIT **22** SKILL WORK ACTIVITY 1a

SOUND PAGE: For use after Story 1

Name _____

77

PROCEDURES

For each step, demonstrate and guide practice as needed.

1. Handwriting—Basic Instructions

- Have students identify the capital letter <u>O</u> as in "Otter."
- Have students trace and write the capital letter <u>O</u>—leaving a finger space between each letter. Repeat with the small letter <u>o</u> on the last two rows.
- In each row, have students circle their best letter.

2. Coloring—Basic Instructions

- Have students color the picture of the otter, using at least three colors.

Note: Neat work helps students take pride in their efforts. Periodically, demonstrate how to produce "neat" work. Show students how to color in one direction and how to color the background. With individuals, comment on best efforts and improvements.

★ **FACT SHEET**

Use work pages from the workbook.

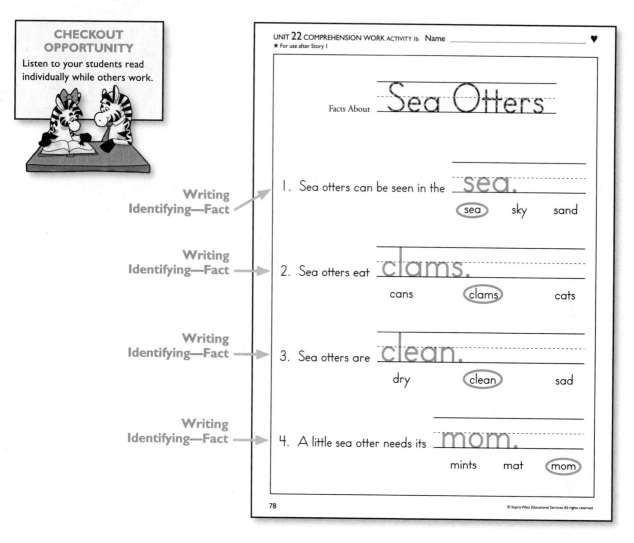

CHECKOUT OPPORTUNITY

Listen to your students read individually while others work.

UNIT **22** COMPREHENSION WORK ACTIVITY 1b   Name _____
★ For use after Story 1

Facts About <u>Sea Otters</u>

Writing
Identifying—Fact

1. Sea otters can be seen in the <u>sea.</u>
   (sea)   sky   sand

Writing
Identifying—Fact

2. Sea otters eat clams.
   cans   (clams)   cats

Writing
Identifying—Fact

3. Sea otters are clean.
   dry   (clean)   sad

Writing
Identifying—Fact

4. A little sea otter needs its mom.
   mints   mat   (mom)

78

PROCEDURES

For each step, demonstrate and guide practice as needed.

- (Demonstrate) Have students orally respond to items while you demonstrate how to complete the page.
- (Guide) Have students orally respond to the items, but do not demonstrate how to complete the page.
- (Independent With Support) Have students silently read over the items and ask any questions they may have.

Multiple Choice, Sentence Completion—Basic Instructions

- Remind students that a fact is something that is real. Tell them they are going to be writing facts about sea otters.
- Have students select and circle the word that correctly completes the sentence. Periodically, think aloud with students. Discuss the multiple choice options. As appropriate, ask questions like: "Does the first answer make sense?" "Is that what the book said?" "Is the answer completely correct?"
- Have them write answers in the blanks and place a period at the end.

Note: You may wish to remind students that they can look in their storybooks if they are unsure about the correct answer.

SOLO STORY READING INSTRUCTIONS
Students read from their own storybooks.

COMPREHENSION BUILDING:
DISCUSSION QUESTIONS AND TEACHER THINK ALOUDS

- Ask questions and discuss text on the first reading when indicated in the storybook in light gray text.
- Encourage students to answer questions with complete sentences.
- If students have difficulty with a comprehension question, think aloud with them or reread the portion of the story that answers the question. Then, ask the question again.

PROCEDURES

1. Review headings in Chapter 1.

Have students turn to Chapter 1. Quickly review a few of the underlined headings and what students learned.

2. First Reading

Mix group and individual turns on student-read sentences. On individual turns, gently correct any error, and then have the student reread the text.

After students complete the first reading and before the second reading, have students practice a paragraph. First demonstrate expressive reading for students, then give individual turns. Acknowledge student efforts.

3. Second Reading

- Mix group and individual turns, independent of your voice.
  Have students work toward an accuracy goal of 0–2 errors.
  Quietly keep track of errors made by all students in each group.
- After reading the story, practice any difficult words.
- If the group has not reached the accuracy goal, have the group reread the story, mixing group and individual turns.

4. Repeated Readings

   a. Timed Readings

- Once the accuracy goal has been achieved, have individual students read the page while the other children track the text with their fingers and whisper read.
  Time individuals for 30 seconds and encourage each student to work for his or her personal best.
- Count the number of words read correctly in 30 seconds (words read minus errors).
  Multiply by two to determine words read correctly per minute. Record student scores.

Note: If a student is unable to read with close to 100% accuracy, the personal goal should be accuracy. If the student is unable to read with accuracy, evaluate group placement and consider a Jell-Well Review.

   b. Partner Reading

During students' daily independent work, have them do Partner Reading.

   c. Homework 1

Have students read the story at home. (A reprint of this story is available on a blackline master in *Read Well* Homework.)

CHAPTER 2

An Otter Eats

HEADINGS

After students read the chapter title, say something like:

Read the heading. (What will the otter do with the clam?)

What will you learn about? (What the otter will do with the clam)

What will the otter do with the clam?

That sweet otter wants to eat that clam. He will hit the clam with a rock. He will hit it hard. With a smack and a whack, that shell will crack.

What does the otter want to eat? **1** How will he crack the clam shell? **2**

31

❶ **Identifying—What** (The otter wants to eat a clam.)

❷ **Explaining** (He will hit it with a rock.)

STORY 2, SOLO

Smack! Whack! That shell did crack. At last the otter has his snack. He will eat his snack at sea. Then he will swim in the sea. He will swish and swoosh in the sea.

Where does the otter eat?**1** Then what does he do?**2**

32

❶ **Identifying—Where** (The otter eats at sea.)
❷ **Identifying—Action** (The otter swims in the sea.)

COMPREHENSION BUILDING: FACT SUMMARY

Read the text. Then, have students orally answer each question. For each question, have students turn back to the matching header in Chapters 1 and 2. Reread the text to affirm student responses.

Otters in the Sea

We learned many facts about sea otters. A fact tells something that is real. Look at the pictures and answer the questions with facts you learned.[1]

1. **What are otters?**[2] Let's check your answer on p. 28.

2. **Where can we see sea otters?**[3] Let's check your answer on p. 29.

3. **How do otters stay warm?**[4] Let's check your answer on p. 29.

4. **What do otters eat?**[5] Let's check your answer on p. 30.

5. **What will the otter do with the clam?**[6] Let's check your answer on p. 31.

6. **What else would you like to learn about otters?**[7]

33

QUESTION 1
Affirming

After answering "What are otters?" have students turn to page 28 in their storybooks. Say something like:

Look at the heading under the picture. What does it say? (What are otters?) That's where we can check our answer. We said otters were mammals. What does it say? (Otters are mammals.) Were we right?

Repeat the process with the other questions as time allows.

❶ **Building Knowledge**

❷ **Classifying** (Otters are mammals.)

❸ **Identifying—Where, Using Vocabulary—Habitat** (We can see otters in the sea. Sea otters live in the sea. Their habitat is the sea.)

❹ **Explaining** (Otters have thick fur. Their fur is made up of millions of hairs.)

❺ **Identifying—What** (Otters eat clams, fish, crab, and sea urchins.)

❻ **Explaining** (The otter will hit the clam with a rock. The otter will break the shell with a rock. Then he will eat the clam.)

❼ **Questioning**

STORY COMPREHENSION

Use work pages from the workbook.

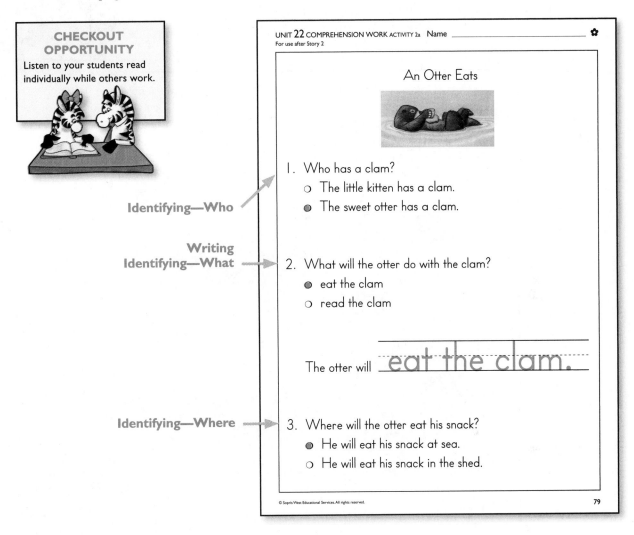

CHECKOUT OPPORTUNITY

Listen to your students read individually while others work.

Identifying—Who

Writing
Identifying—What

Identifying—Where

UNIT **22** COMPREHENSION WORK ACTIVITY 2a   Name _____
For use after Story 2

An Otter Eats

1. Who has a clam?
   - ○ The little kitten has a clam.
   - ● The sweet otter has a clam.

2. What will the otter do with the clam?
   - ● eat the clam
   - ○ read the clam

   The otter will _eat the clam._

3. Where will the otter eat his snack?
   - ● He will eat his snack at sea.
   - ○ He will eat his snack in the shed.

79

PROCEDURES

For each step, demonstrate and guide practice as needed.

Multiple Choice, Sentence Completion—Basic Instructions

- Have students fill in the bubble for the correct answer.
- Have them write an answer in the blank and place a period at the end.

Note: You may wish to remind students that they can look in their storybooks if they are unsure about the correct answer.

ALPHABET DETECTIVE

Use work pages from the workbook.

CHECKOUT OPPORTUNITY
Listen to your students read individually while others work.

PROCEDURES

For each step, demonstrate and guide practice as needed.

1. Letter Find—Basic Instructions

- Have students look at the first box at the top of the page and follow the directions. Ask:

  What letters will you look for? (The capital letter O and the small letter o)

  What will you do when you find a capital letter O or a small letter o? (Draw a triangle around it.)

- Have students look at the second box at the top of the page. Ask:

  What other letter will you look for? (The small letter l)

  What will you do when you find a small letter l? (Circle it.)

2. Self-Monitoring—Basic Instructions

Have students systematically check each line after finishing the task.

Alternative: At the beginning of the exercise, tell students the number of o's they will draw a triangle around and the number of l's they will circle. Have students write the numbers on the top of their papers. When students complete the activity, have them count the number of triangles and circles they have drawn. If the numbers are incorrect, they can recheck each line.

3. Coloring—Optional

Have students carefully color the picture, using at least three colors.

Note: If students have difficulty with the multi-step directions, have them do just the first step.

① SOUND REVIEW

Use selected Sound Cards for Units 1–22 or the Sound Review on Decoding Practice 4.

② NEW SOUND PRACTICE

◆◆ **③ FOCUS ON VOCABULARY**

★ **New vocabulary word: "celebration"**

Introduce the word "celebration" and give examples of its meaning. Say something like:

Your new vocabulary word is "celebration." Tell me your new word. (Celebration)

A *celebration* is often a party. A birthday party is a birthday . . . celebration.

A party to congratulate someone is called a celebration.

After the baseball team won the game, they had a . . . celebration.

④ SOUNDING OUT SMOOTHLY

- For each word, have students say any underlined part, sound out the word, and then read the word. Use the words in sentences as needed.
- Provide repeated practice. Mix group and individual turns, independent of your voice.

Note: For the word "mammal," tell students that they can sound out this big word that is made up of two parts. Have students sound out "mam," then "mal." Remind students that a letter with a slash through it doesn't say anything. Next, have students look at the equals sign. Say something like:

When you put the two little parts together, what big word does it make? (mammal)

Repeat with "camel."

⑤ ACCURACY AND FLUENCY BUILDING

★ **New consonant blend: /tw-/**

- For each column, have students say any underlined part, then read each word.
- Have students read the whole column.
- Repeat practice on each column, building accuracy first and then fluency.

Note: If students have difficulty with /tw-/ in the Triangle Column, write "ist" on the chalkboard and have students read "ist." Add a <u>w</u> and have students read "wist." Then add a <u>t</u> and have students read "twist."

⑥ TRICKY WORDS

★ **New Tricky Word: "Otto"**

- Have students look at their new Tricky Word, "Otto." Say something like:
  Your new Tricky Word is "Otto." Otto is the name of an otter in your story.
  We spell "Otto" <u>O-t-t-o</u>. Spell "Otto" with me. <u>O-t-t-o</u>
  Spell "Otto" three times by yourselves. (<u>O-t-t-o</u>, <u>O-t-t-o</u>, <u>O-t-t-o</u>)
  Touch the word "Otto" and read it. (Otto) The otter in our story is named . . . Otto.
- Have students read the row. Repeat, mixing group and individual turns.

⑦ DAILY STORY READING

Proceed to the Unit 22 Storybook. See Daily Lesson Planning for pacing suggestions.

⑧ COMPREHENSION AND SKILL WORK ACTIVITY 3 AND/OR ACTIVITY 4

See pages 35 and/or 39.

◆◆ For ELLs and children with language delays, provide repeated and extended practice with the language patterns. See page 10 for tips.

UNIT **22** DECODING PRACTICE 2
(For use with Stories 3 and 4)

▲

1. SOUND REVIEW Use Sound Cards for Units 1–22 or Sound Review on Decoding Practice 4.

2. NEW SOUND PRACTICE Have students read, trace, and say /ooo/.

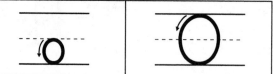

★3. FOCUS ON VOCABULARY Introduce "celebration." See the Teacher's Guide for detailed instructions.

4. SOUNDING OUT SMOOTHLY For each word, have students say any underlined part, sound out the word in one smooth breath, and then read the word.

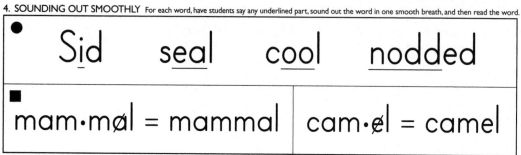

● S<u>i</u>d   s<u>ea</u>l   c<u>oo</u>l   n<u>o</u>dd<u>e</u>d

■ mam·m⌀l = mammal | cam·⌀l = camel

★5. ACCURACY/FLUENCY BUILDING For each column, have students say any underlined part, then read each word. Next, have students read the column.

▲	✈	✿
★tw<u>i</u>st	m<u>o</u>m	wet
tr<u>ea</u>t	n<u>o</u>t	let
sl<u>ee</u>k	R<u>o</u>d	lend
clams		land

★6. TRICKY WORDS Introduce "Otto" using the Tricky Word procedure. Next, have students silently figure out each word and then read it aloud.

♥ ★Otto   otters   Who   there

7. DAILY STORY READING

50

Sentence Suggestions: Use the appropriate suggested sentence *after* decoding each individual word.

DUET STORY READING INSTRUCTIONS

Students read from their own storybooks.

The teacher reads the small text and students read the large text.

PACING

- 2- to 4-Day Plans: Have students do the first reading of Duet Story 3.

  Then, proceed to repeated readings of Solo Story 4.
- 6- to 10-Day Plans: Have students do the first *and* second readings as needed.

COMPREHENSION BUILDING: DISCUSSION QUESTIONS AND TEACHER THINK ALOUDS

- Ask questions and discuss text on the first reading when indicated in the storybook in light gray text.
- Encourage students to answer questions with complete sentences.
- If students have difficulty with a comprehension question, think aloud with them or reread the portion of the story that answers the question. Then, ask the question again.

PROCEDURES

1. First Reading

Mix group and individual turns on student-read sentences. On individual turns, gently correct any error, and then have the student reread the text.

2. Second Reading

Repeat the reading only as needed for comprehension.

Otto's First Birthday Celebration

What is a celebration? **1** What is Otto celebrating? **2**

CHAPTER I

A Scavenger Hunt

What a great day! It was Otto's birthday, and his friends had gathered for a party. This was Otto's first party. Otto was a little nervous, but things had gone well. The little otters played Pin the Fin on the Fish and Go Fish.

At last, Otto's mom said, "I have a surprise for you. We have one more game to play. It's a scavenger hunt. You get to be detectives."

The little otters said, "That's cool!

That's neat! What do we do?"

Otto's mom said, "There are clues to follow. Follow the clues. At the end of the scavenger hunt, you will find a treat that can't be beat."

Otto said, "A treat! Is it clams?"

"Not clams," said Otto's mom.

What will the otters find at the end of the scavenger hunt? **3** That's their goal—to find the treat. **4**

34

FOCUS ON VOCABULARY
Making Connections
After completing the page, say something like: The otters are going to be detectives in this game. A detective finds things. What are the otters going to find? (They are going to find a treat.)

They will follow clues. What is a clue? (A clue is something that helps us find something.)

That sounds like a fun game. Have you ever played a game with clues?

❶ Defining Vocabulary—Celebration (A celebration is a party to congratulate someone.)

❷ Identifying—What (His first birthday)

❸ Identifying—Goal (The otters will find a treat.)

❹ Teacher Think Aloud

Otto's mom said, "Read this card."

The card said:

This is your first clue. Go find a mammal.

It isn't a camel!

We see this mammal

on the land *and* in the sea.

This big creature has one strange feature—
its very large nose!

Who can it be?

Listen again.
What do the otters need
to look for?**1** That's the
first clue.**2**

35

❶ **Identifying—What** (A mammal that lives on the land and in the sea.)

❷ **Teacher Think Aloud, Using Vocabulary—Clue**

STORY 3, DUET

"This is fun," said Tess. "The clue is like a puzzle piece. An elephant has a very large nose, but an elephant doesn't live in the sea."

Rod nodded. Then he said, "We need to think. This is hard!"

Otto said, "A whale is a mammal. It lives in the sea, but it doesn't live on the land. And, it doesn't have a large nose."

How does Otto know they aren't looking for a whale?[1]

36

❶ **Explaining** (It doesn't live on the land; it doesn't have a large nose.)

Then Tess said, "I think it's a seal!"

"It's not a seal," said Rod. "A seal doesn't have a big nose."

Why does Rod think it isn't a seal?[1]

Then Otto said, "I think it is a seal.

We need to see Sid Seal. Follow me."

For some reason, Otto thinks they are looking for a seal.[2] What do you think Otto knows about Sid Seal?[3]

> **VISUALIZING**
> After reading the page, say something like: Close your eyes. Imagine the seals you've seen. Does the seal you are thinking of have a big nose? Otto thinks the clue is about Sid Seal. Do you think he is on the right track?

37

❶ Explaining (Most seals don't have big noses.)

❷ Teacher Think Aloud

❸ Predicting, Inferring

STORY COMPREHENSION

Use work pages from the workbook.

Identifying—Who

Identifying—What

Writing
Identifying—Who

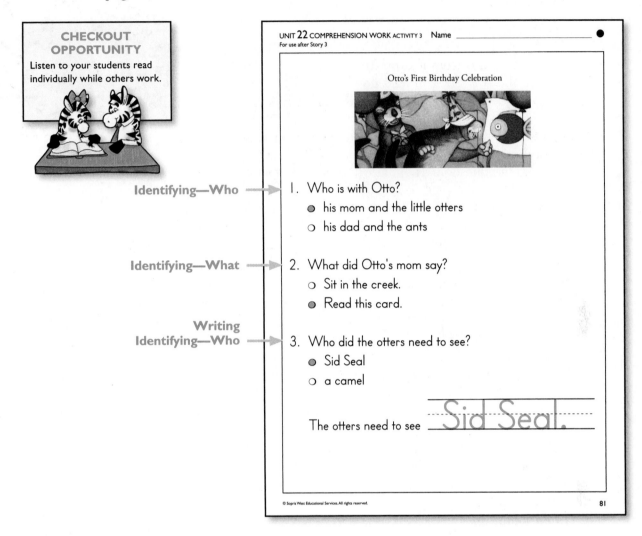

UNIT **22** COMPREHENSION WORK ACTIVITY 3   Name _____

For use after Story 3

Otto's First Birthday Celebration

1. Who is with Otto?
   ● his mom and the little otters
   ○ his dad and the ants

2. What did Otto's mom say?
   ○ Sit in the creek.
   ● Read this card.

3. Who did the otters need to see?
   ● Sid Seal
   ○ a camel

   The otters need to see _Sid Seal._

81

PROCEDURES

For each step, demonstrate and guide practice as needed.

Multiple Choice, Sentence Completion—Basic Instructions

- Have students fill in the bubble for the correct answer.
- Have them write an answer in the blank and place a period at the end.

Note: You may wish to remind students that they can look in their storybooks if they are unsure about the correct answer.

SOLO STORY READING INSTRUCTIONS

Students read from their own storybooks.

COMPREHENSION BUILDING:
DISCUSSION QUESTIONS AND TEACHER THINK ALOUDS

- Ask questions and discuss text on the first reading when indicated in the storybook in light gray text.
- Encourage students to answer questions with complete sentences.
- If students have difficulty with a comprehension question, think aloud with them or reread the portion of the story that answers the question. Then, ask the question again.

PROCEDURES

1. First Reading

- Mix group and individual turns on student-read sentences. On individual turns, gently correct any error, and then have the student reread the text.
- After students complete the first reading and before the second reading, have students practice a paragraph. First demonstrate expressive reading for students, then give individual turns. Acknowledge student efforts.

2. Second Reading

- Mix group and individual turns, independent of your voice. Have students work toward an accuracy goal of 0–2 errors. Quietly keep track of errors made by all students in each group.
- After reading the story, practice any difficult words.
- If the group has not reached the accuracy goal, have the group reread the story, mixing group and individual turns.

3. Repeated Readings
a. Timed Readings

- Once the accuracy goal has been achieved, have individual students read the page while the other children track the text with their fingers and whisper read.

Time individuals for 30 seconds and encourage each student to work for his or her personal best.

- Count the number of words read correctly in 30 seconds (words read minus errors). Multiply by two to determine words read correctly per minute. Record student scores.

b. Partner Reading

During students' daily independent work, have them do Partner Reading.

c. Homework 2

Have students read the story at home. (A reprint of this story is available on a blackline master in *Read Well* Homework.)

STORY 4, SOLO

CHAPTER 2
Meet the Seals

Remember, the otters are on a scavenger hunt. **I**What are they looking for?**2**

Otto was sleek and swam well.
He swam with a whoosh and a swoosh.
He could twist in the wet sea.

Soon Otto could see rocks in the sea. Otto said, "Look! See the seals on the rocks."

The little otters nodded. A little seal swam to meet them.

38

❶ Summarizing

❷ Identifying—What, Who (They are looking for clues that will lead them to a treat; they are looking for Sid Seal.)

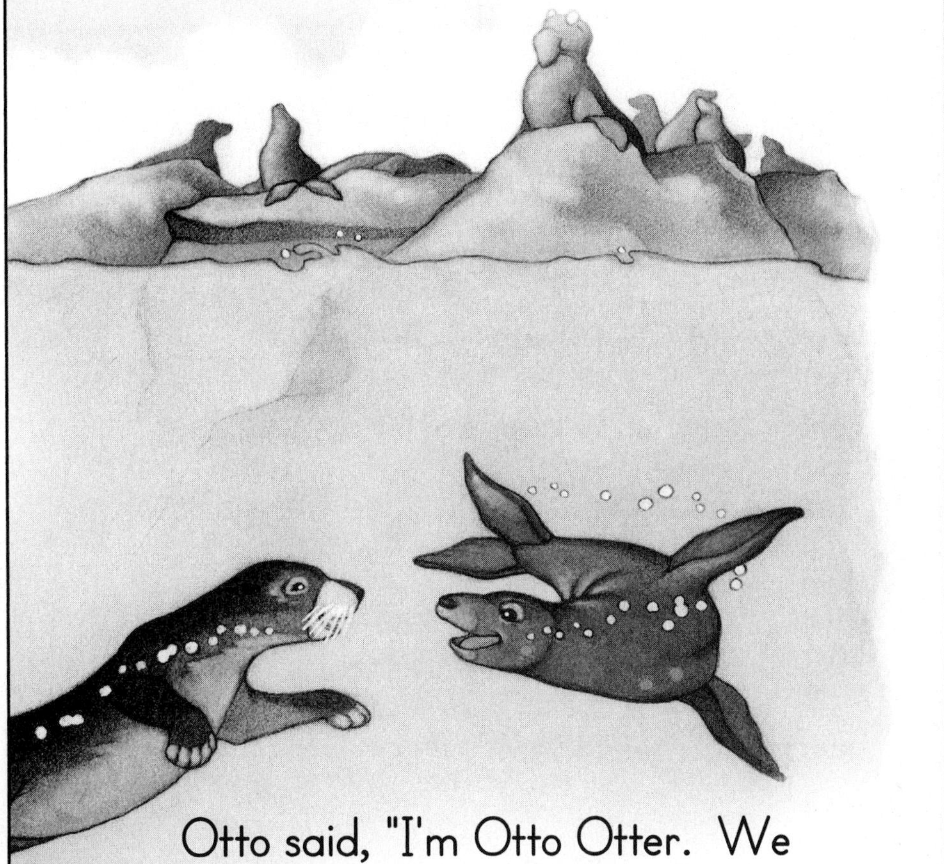

Otto said, "I'm Otto Otter. We need to see Sid Seal."

The little seal said, "That's cool. Sid is my dad. He is on the rocks. Let's swim to the rocks."

Why do the otters want to see the little seal's dad?**1** What do they hope to find at the end of the scavenger hunt?**2** That's their goal—to find a treat.**3**

39

❶ Inferring (They hope he has a clue for them.)

❷ Identifying—Goal (They hope to find a treat.)

❸ Teacher Think Aloud

RHYMING PATTERNS

Use work pages from the workbook.

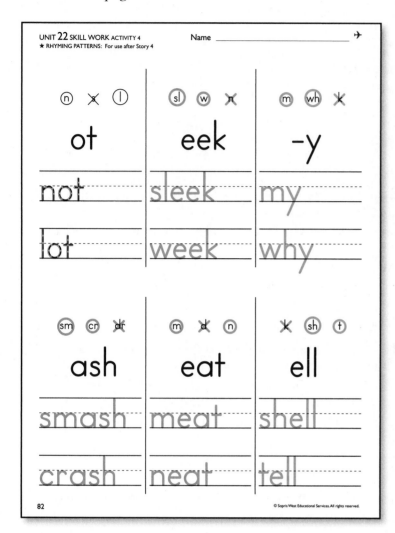

UNIT 22 SKILL WORK ACTIVITY 4
★ RHYMING PATTERNS: For use after Story 4   Name _____

ⓝ ✗ ⓛ   ⓢˡ ⓦ ✗   ⓜ ⓦʰ ✗

ot   eek   -y

not   sleek   my

lot   week   why

ⓢᵐ ⓒʳ ✗   ⓜ ✗ ⓝ   ✗ ⓢʰ ⓣ

ash   eat   ell

smash   meat   shell

crash   neat   tell

82   © Sopris West Educational Services. All rights reserved.

CHECKOUT OPPORTUNITY

Listen to your students read individually while others work.

PROCEDURES

Demonstrate and guide practice as needed.

Rhyming Patterns—Basic Instructions

For each box, have students:

- Read the rhyming pattern.
- Circle the two sounds above the rhyming pattern that go with it to make real words.
- Cross out the sound that does not make a real word with the rhyming pattern.
- Write the two rhyming words on the lines provided.

Note: For students who struggle or who lack the English language base to know which are real words, you may wish to identify the two sounds they should circle in each box. Students can then write the pattern words on their own.

1 SOUND REVIEW

2 NEW SOUND PRACTICE

◆◆ **3 FOCUS ON VOCABULARY**

Review vocabulary word: "celebration"

Have students review the word "celebration" and use it in a sentence. Say something like:
Remember, a celebration is often a . . . party.
When you graduated from [kindergarten], you had a graduation . . . (celebration).
When people have birthdays, sometimes they have a birthday . . . (celebration).

◆◆ **4 SOUNDING OUT SMOOTHLY**

- For each word, have students say the underlined part, sound out the word, and then read the word. Use the words in sentences as needed.
- Provide repeated practice. Mix group and individual turns, independent of your voice.

5 ACCURACY AND FLUENCY BUILDING

- For each column, have students say any underlined part, then read each word.
- Have students read the whole column.
- Repeat practice on each column, building accuracy first and then fluency.

Note: After students read the Airplane Column, ask them what is the same about "crack," "smack," "snack," and "whack." (They rhyme. They all end with /-ack/.)

6 TRICKY WORDS

⭐ - Have students look at their new Tricky Word, "Listen." Remind them that a letter with a slash through it doesn't say anything.
- Have students sound out the word.
- Have students read the word three times and use it in a sentence.
- Have students read the row. Repeat, mixing group and individual turns, independent of your voice.

7 DAILY STORY READING

Proceed to the Unit 22 Storybook. See Daily Lesson Planning for pacing suggestions.

8 COMPREHENSION AND SKILL WORK ACTIVITY 5 AND/OR ACTIVITY 6

See pages 47 and/or 51.

◆◆ For ELLs and children with language delays, provide repeated and extended practice with the language patterns. See page 10 for tips.

40

UNIT **22** DECODING PRACTICE 3
(For use with Stories 5 and 6)

●

1. SOUND REVIEW Use Sound Cards for Units 1–22 or Sound Review on Decoding Practice 4.

2. NEW SOUND PRACTICE Have students read, trace, and say /ooo/.

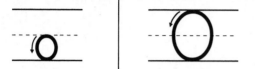

3. FOCUS ON VOCABULARY Review "celebration."
See the Teacher's Guide for detailed instructions.

4. SOUNDING OUT SMOOTHLY For each word, have students say the underlined part, sound out the word in one smooth breath, and then read the word.

■ n<u>o</u>t   r<u>o</u>cks   <u>on</u>   m<u>o</u>m

● T<u>e</u>ss   l<u>a</u>st   h<u>i</u>dden   s<u>ea</u>ls

5. ACCURACY/FLUENCY BUILDING For each column, have students say any underlined part, then read each word. Next, have students read the column.

✈	✐	❀
cr<u>ack</u>	h<u>oo</u>t	will
smack	sh<u>oo</u>t	well
snack	<u>shoots</u>	swell
whack		shell

6. TRICKY WORDS Have students silently figure out each word and then read it aloud.

♥ ★Lis<u>t</u>en   Where   Otto's   littl<u>e</u>

7. DAILY STORY READING

51

Sentence Suggestions: Use the appropriate suggested sentence *after* decoding each individual word.

DUET STORY READING INSTRUCTIONS

Students read from their own storybooks.

The teacher reads the small text and students read the large text.

PACING

- 2- to 4-Day Plans: Have students do the first reading of Duet Story 5.

  Then proceed to repeated readings of Solo Story 6.
- 6- to 10-Day Plans: Have students do the first *and* second readings as needed.

COMPREHENSION BUILDING:
DISCUSSION QUESTIONS AND TEACHER THINK ALOUDS

- Ask questions and discuss text on the first reading when indicated in the storybook in light gray text.
- Encourage students to answer questions with complete sentences.
- If students have difficulty with a comprehension question, think aloud with them or reread the portion of the story that answers the question. Then, ask the question again.

PROCEDURES

1. First Reading

Mix group and individual turns on student-read sentences. On individual turns, gently correct any error, and then have the student reread the text.

2. Second Reading

Repeat the reading only as needed for comprehension.

STORY 5, DUET

CHAPTER 3

A Seal With a Big Nose

Remember, the otters are on a scavenger hunt.¹ What do they want to find?²

In no time at all the little seal and the otters were climbing onto the rocks in search of Sid.

At last the little seal said, "This is my dad, Sid." At that, the little otters nodded. Sid was an elephant seal. Like other male elephant seals, Sid had a great big nose.

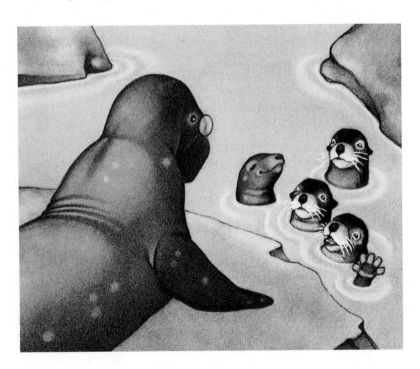

Do you think the otters have found their next clue?³ Is Sid a mammal that lives on the land and in the sea?⁴ Does he have a big nose?⁵

40

VISUALIZING

After discussing the gray questions at the top of the page, have students imagine the mammal the little seals are looking for. Say something like: Remember, the clue said the little otters were looking for a mammal that lives on the land and the sea.

Otto thinks it is a seal. Does a seal live on the land and in the sea? (Yes)

The clue also said the mammal had a very big nose. Close your eyes and imagine a seal with a very big nose.

Now look at the picture. Does that seal have a big nose?

❶ **Teacher Think Aloud—Summarizing**

❷ **Identifying—Goal** (A treat)

❸ **Inferring, Using Vocabulary—Clue**

❹ **Applying** (Yes)

❺ **Applying** (Yes)

Sid waddled over to meet the little otters. The otters and seals exchanged pleasantries for a bit.

Then Sid Seal said, "Otto's mom said I should read this card."

The little otters nodded. Sid said,

"Listen. This clue will help you find your treat."

This is what the next clue said:

Dear Little Otter Detectives,

You did swell.
I hope this note finds you well.

Search the sea for this creature.
She has a really special feature.

She shoots ink when she's scared,
And changes color when she's dared.

She has eight legs as a rule.
This creature is really cool.

—Otto's Mom

What were the clues in the note?[1]

Tess said, "That's strange. I can't think of a mammal with eight legs."

VISUALIZING

After reading the page, say something like: Close your eyes and listen to me read the clue again. Imagine what the little otters are looking for.

What do you think they are looking for?

41

❶ **Identifying—What, Using Vocabulary—Clue** (The clues were to look for a sea creature that shoots ink, changes color, and has eight legs.)

44

Rod said, "It is not a mammal."

Then Tess said, "Not a mammal?

Tee hee. I see. Then this isn't hard.

She shoots ink. She has eight legs! It's got to be Grandmother Octopus!"

One little seal joined in the search.

At last Tess said, "There she is. She is

hidden in the rocks, and she has a card."

With that, Grandmother Octopus slid from the rocks. "Welcome," she said. "I've been waiting for you. I also have a clue to read to you."

42

This is what the card said:

> Dear Little Detectives:
>
> You've done swell.
> I'm glad you're well.
>
> For your treat, I did bake,
> One terrific crab cake.
>
>   —Otto's Mom
> P.S. All you need to do is find me.

What was the surprise?[1] Where do you think the otters and the seal will find the crab cake?[2]

Otto said with pride, "Mom's crab cake is the best!"

What was the treat?[3] What do you think the little otters will do next?[4]

43

[1] **Identifying—What** (A crab cake)

[2] **Inferring, Predicting** (The crab cake will be back at Otto's house with his mom.)

[3] **Identifying—What** (The treat was a crab cake.)

[4] **Predicting**

STORY COMPREHENSION

Use work pages from the workbook.

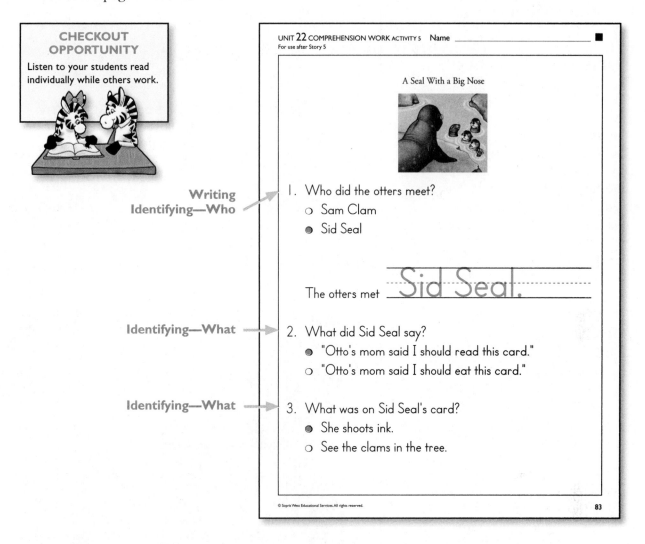

UNIT **22** COMPREHENSION WORK ACTIVITY 5   Name _____ ■
For use after Story 5

A Seal With a Big Nose

Writing
Identifying—Who

1. Who did the otters meet?
   ○ Sam Clam
   ● Sid Seal

The otters met _Sid Seal._

Identifying—What

2. What did Sid Seal say?
   ● "Otto's mom said I should read this card."
   ○ "Otto's mom said I should eat this card."

Identifying—What

3. What was on Sid Seal's card?
   ● She shoots ink.
   ○ See the clams in the tree.

83

PROCEDURES

For each step, demonstrate and guide practice as needed.

Multiple Choice, Sentence Completion—Basic Instructions
   • Have students fill in the bubble for the correct answer.
   • Have them write an answer in the blank and place a period at the end.

Note: You may wish to remind students that they can look in their storybooks if they are unsure about the correct answer.

SOLO STORY READING INSTRUCTIONS

Students read from their own storybooks.

COMPREHENSION BUILDING: DISCUSSION QUESTIONS AND TEACHER THINK ALOUDS

- Ask questions and discuss text on the first reading when indicated in the storybook in light gray text.
- Encourage students to answer questions with complete sentences.
- If students have difficulty with a comprehension question, think aloud with them or reread the portion of the story that answers the question. Then, ask the question again.

PROCEDURES

1. First Reading

- Mix group and individual turns on student-read sentences. On individual turns, gently correct any error, and then have the student reread the text.
- After students complete the first reading and before the second reading, have students practice a paragraph. First demonstrate expressive reading for students, then give individual turns. Acknowledge student efforts.

STORY 6, SOLO

CHAPTER 4

At Otto's

What did the seal and otters want to find?[1] Where did they go?[2]

Soon Otto's mom said, "Read my last card." The card said:

Who wants to eat this treat?

44

❶ **Summarizing, Identifying—Goal** (The seal and otters wanted to find the treat.)

❷ **Identifying—Where** (They went back to Otto's home.)

2. Second Reading

- Mix group and individual turns, independent of your voice. Have students work toward an accuracy goal of 0–2 errors. Quietly keep track of errors made by all students in each group.
- After reading the story, practice any difficult words.
- If the group has not reached the accuracy goal, have the group reread the story, mixing group and individual turns.

3. Repeated Readings
a. Timed Readings

- Once the accuracy goal has been achieved, have individual students read the page while the other children track the text with their fingers and whisper read. Time individuals for 30 seconds and encourage each student to work for his or her personal best.
- Count the number of words read correctly in 30 seconds (words read minus errors). Multiply by two to determine words read correctly per minute. Record student scores.

b. Partner Reading

During students' daily independent work, have them do Partner Reading.

c. Homework 3

Have students read the story at home. (A reprint of this story is available on a blackline master in *Read Well* Homework.)

STORY 6, SOLO

"I do," said the seal.

"We do," said the otters.

"Me too," said Otto.

I think the little sea mammals deserve their treat.**1** What do you think?**2** Were they having fun?**3**

45

❶ **Teacher Think Aloud**

❷ **Inferring**

❸ **Inferring**

"Well then," said Otto's mom. "Let's eat this treat!"

Soon Otto's mom could hear, "Smack, smack, smack. What a sweet treat!"

The little seal said, "Otto, this was cool. Thanks!"

The little otters said, "Otto, this was neat. Thanks!"

Then Otto said, "Thanks to my mom. Thanks, Mom, thanks!"

Why did Otto thank his mom?[1] Did Otto have a good birthday?[2]

46

[1] **Inferring, Making Connections** (She made him a crab cake; she gave him a party.)
[2] **Inferring**

SENTENCE COMPREHENSION

Use work pages from the workbook.

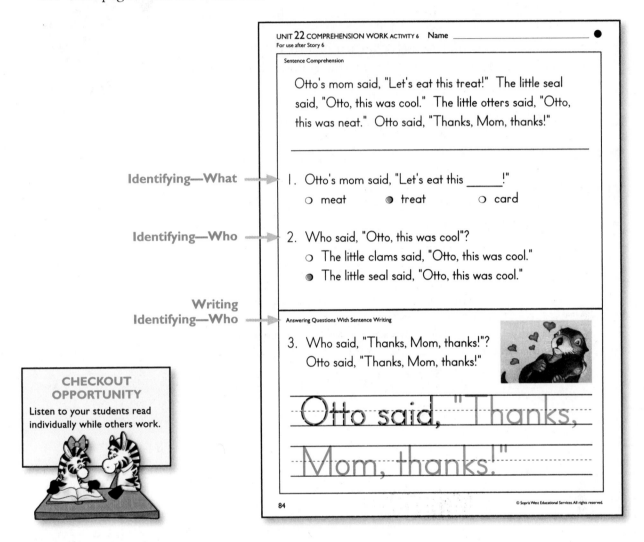

UNIT 22 COMPREHENSION WORK ACTIVITY 6 Name _____
For use after Story 6

Sentence Comprehension

Otto's mom said, "Let's eat this treat!" The little seal said, "Otto, this was cool." The little otters said, "Otto, this was neat." Otto said, "Thanks, Mom, thanks!"

_____

Identifying—What → 1. Otto's mom said, "Let's eat this _____!"
  ○ meat   ● treat   ○ card

Identifying—Who → 2. Who said, "Otto, this was cool"?
  ○ The little clams said, "Otto, this was cool."
  ● The little seal said, "Otto, this was cool."

Writing
Identifying—Who → Answering Questions With Sentence Writing

3. Who said, "Thanks, Mom, thanks!"?
Otto said, "Thanks, Mom, thanks!"

Otto said, "Thanks, Mom, thanks!"

84   © Sopris West Educational Services. All rights reserved.

CHECKOUT OPPORTUNITY

Listen to your students read individually while others work.

PROCEDURES

For each step, demonstrate and guide practice as needed.

1. Sentence Comprehension, Multiple Choice—Basic Instructions

Have students read the sentences and answer the questions.

2. Answering Questions With Sentence Writing—Basic Instructions

- Have students read the question and answer.
- Have students trace the beginning of the sentence and complete the sentence.

Note: You may wish to remind students that a sentence begins with a capital and ends with a period.

Note: There are multiple uses for Decoding Practice 4.
- Use the Sound Review rows in place of Sound Card Practice.
- Use the whole page at the end of the unit for fluency building and/or to informally assess skills.
- Have students complete the page as a partner review.
- Build spelling dictation lessons from the sounds and words on this page.

① SOUND REVIEW

② ACCURACY AND FLUENCY BUILDING

③ TRICKY WORDS

④ DAILY STORY READING

See Daily Lesson Planning for story suggestions.

WORDS CONVEY MEANING

As students learn to decode words, your attention to meaning will help students make connections with the words they are reading.

• Throughout the decoding lessons, use the words students are reading in sentences.

• Have students use the words in sentences.

• Ask students what the words mean.

UNIT 22 DECODING PRACTICE 4
(See Daily Lesson Planning for story suggestions.)

1. SOUND REVIEW Demonstrate an appropriate pace. Have students read the sounds in each row.

■	O	c	h	ar	L	ea	r	7
❀	-y	T	oo	w	i	d	a	14
♥	Sh	ĕ	m	o	k	l	ee	21

2. ACCURACY/FLUENCY BUILDING For each column, have students say any underlined part, then read each word. Next, have students read the column.

✈	✈✈	❀	❀❀	❀❀❀
h<u>ot</u>	w<u>ell</u>	cost	l<u>i</u>ttle	clean
tot	swell	lost	s<u>e</u>ttle	clock
lot	shell	loss	r<u>a</u>ttle	clam
cot	smell	m<u>o</u>ss	d<u>oo</u>dle	slam
dot	tell	moth	n<u>ee</u>dle	sleek

> **RECOGNIZING RIMES**
> **(Reminder)**
> Recognition of the common visual patterns in the words helps facilitate speed of word recognition. The Airplane Columns help students chunk these rimes. With each reading of a column, increase the pace.
>
> Say something like:
> I think you can read the first airplane column about this fast . . . hot, tot, lot. Now it's your turn to read the whole column.

3. TRICKY WORDS Have students silently figure out each word and then read it aloud.

| ☆☆ | listen | one | into | could | What | 5 |
| ☆☆ | there | look | hasn't | two | was | 10 |

4. DAILY STORY READING

End of the Unit

In this section, you will find:

Making Decisions

As you near the end of the unit, you will need to make decisions. Should you administer the Oral Reading Fluency Assessment or should you teach Extra Practice lessons?

Unit 22 Oral Reading Fluency Assessment

The Unit 22 Oral Reading Fluency Assessment is located on page 56 and can also be found in the *Assessment Manual*.

Certificate of Achievement

Celebrate your children's accomplishments.

Extra Practice

Lessons and blackline masters for added decoding practice and independent work are provided for students who need extended practice opportunities.

Making Decisions

ASSESSMENT READINESS

Assess when students are able to easily complete decoding tasks from the beginning of a lesson.

- If you aren't sure whether students are ready for the assessment, give the assessment. Do Extra Practice lessons if needed.
- If students are not ready for the assessment, proceed to Extra Practice lessons. Administer the assessment as soon as students are ready.

GENERAL ASSESSMENT GUIDELINES

- Assess all students.
- Assess each child individually.
- Score student responses on the Student Assessment Record, adhering to the scoring criteria in the *Assessment Manual*. Use a stopwatch to time how long it takes the student to read the oral fluency passage.
- Follow the general instructions at the bottom of each assessment. Record a Strong Pass, a Weak Pass, or a No Pass.

ACCELERATION

- If students read with 100% accuracy and exceed the fluency goal, consider shortening units.
- If an individual student reads with greater fluency than others in his or her group, consider regrouping.

INTERVENTION OPTIONS—INDIVIDUALS

1. Add informal practice throughout the day.
2. Add practice with repeated readings on Solo Stories.
3. Find ways to provide a double dose of *Read Well* instruction.
   - Have the student work in his or her group *and* a lower group.
   - Have an instructional assistant, older student, or parent volunteer preview or review lessons.
   - Have an instructional assistant provide instruction with Extra Practice lessons.
4. Consider placement in a lower group. If one child's fluency scores are significantly lower than the other children in the group, success will be impossible without additional and intensive practice.

INTERVENTION OPTIONS—GROUP

1. Extend the unit with Extra Practice lessons.
2. Consider a Jell-Well Review before moving forward. (See the *Assessment Manual*.)

CERTIFICATE OF ACHIEVEMENT

When students pass the assessment, celebrate with the Certificate of Achievement. Then, set a personal goal. (See *Getting Started*.)

TRICKY WORD WARM-UP

two	his	should	wanted	there

ORAL READING FLUENCY PASSAGE

A Nest

★ What do we see? We see a nest.   8

Where is that nest? It's in the tree.   16

Where is that tree? It is on a rock.   25

Where is that rock? It's not on land.   33

It is in the sea.   38

ORAL READING FLUENCY	Start timing at the ★ Mark errors. Make a single slash in the text (/) at 60 seconds. Have student complete passage. If the student completes the passage in less than 60 seconds, have the student go back to the ★ and continue reading. Make a double slash (//) in the text at 60 seconds.
WCPM	Determine words correct per minute by subtracting errors from words read in 60 seconds.
STRONG PASS	The student scores no more than 2 errors on the first pass through the passage and reads a minimum of 52 or more words correct per minute. Proceed to Unit 23.
WEAK PASS	The student scores no more than 2 errors on the first pass through the passage and reads 41 to 51 words correct per minute. Proceed to Unit 23 with added fluency practice, or provide Extra Practice lessons in Unit 22, and/or provide a Jell-Well Review.
NO PASS	The student scores 3 or more errors on the first pass through the passage and/or reads 40 or fewer words correct per minute. Provide Extra Practice lessons and retest, and/or provide a Jell-Well Review.

Certificate of Achievement

This certifies that

_____ ,

on this _____ day of _____ , ____ ,

has successfully completed

Read Well Unit 22

Sounds Mastered: s, e, ee, m, a, d, th, n, t, w, i, Th, h, c, r, ea, sh, k, -ck, oo, ar, wh, ĕ, -y (as in "fly"), l, o

Known Words: By Unit 21, you had learned and practiced 347 words.

New Words Mastered in Unit 22: camel, listen, mammal, mammals, otter, otters, Otto, Otto's, clam, clams, clean, clock, cost, cot, doodle, dot, hidden, hot, lend, loss, lost, lot, mom, moss, moth, needle, nodded, not, on, rattle, rock, rocks, Rod, seal, seals, settle, shell, shoots, slam, sleek, smooth, Tess, tot, twist

You can now read 391 words—plus many other words made up of the sounds and patterns you've learned.

te: Personal and Team Goal Setting forms can be copied from Units 16 and 17, or from *Getting Started*.

① SOUNDS

Have students say each sound.

② WORD DICTATION

Have students count the sounds in each word with their fingers, identify and write each sound, and then read the word. Use the words in sentences as needed.

we, tree, and, land

The first word is "we." Tell me the word. (we)
We're going to count the sounds in "we."
Tell me the first sound. **Hold up one finger.** (/www/)
Tell me the next sound. **Hold up two fingers.** (/eee/)
How many sounds are in "we"? (Two)

Tell me the first sound. (/www/) Write it.
Tell me the next sound. (/eee/) Write it.
Do Smooth Blending. (/wwweee/) Read the word. (we)

Repeat with "tree," "and," and "land."

③ SENTENCE COMPLETION

That is not a *rock*.

- Have students read the beginning of the sentence with you.
- Dictate the last word "rock."
- Have students trace the dotted words and complete the sentence with a period.
- Have students read the sentence.

④ ACCURACY AND FLUENCY BUILDING

- For each column, have students say any underlined part, then read each word.
- Have students read the whole column.
- Repeat practice on each column, building accuracy first and then fluency.

⑤ TRICKY WORDS

Repeat practice, mixing group and individual turns, independent of your voice.

⑥ DAILY STORY READING

Proceed to Extra Practice Activity 1.

- Have students read each sentence from the book.
- Repeat, mixing group and individual turns, independent of your voice.

⑦ EXTRA PRACTICE ACTIVITY 1—CHECKOUT OPPORTUNITY

Have students fold, color, and read the book.

CAUTION

Your children may not need Extra Practice. If in doubt, assess students and include Extra Practice only if needed.

DICTATION

- Demonstrate and guide practice as needed.
- Have students check and correct.

BUILDING MASTERY (Reminder)

Throughout Extra Practice, demonstrate and guide practice, but only as needed.

Name_____

1. SOUNDS Have students say each sound.

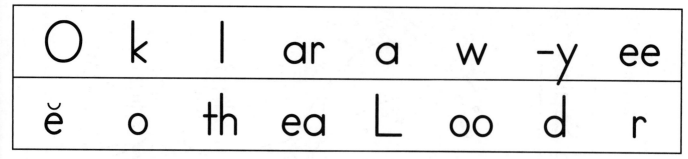

O	k	l	ar	a	w	-y	ee
ĕ	o	th	ea	L	oo	d	r

2. WORD DICTATION Have students count the sounds in each word, identify and write each sound, and then read the word: "we," "tree," "and," and "land."

1 _____ 2 _____ 3 _____ 4 _____

3. SENTENCE COMPLETION Have students read the beginning of the sentence. Dictate "rock." Have students trace the words and complete the sentence with a period.

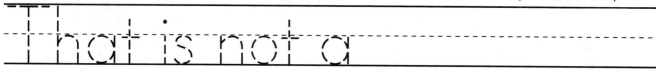

That is not a

4. ACCURACY/FLUENCY BUILDING In each column, have students say any underlined part, then read each word. Next, have students read the column.

♥	♥♥	♥♥♥
<u>o</u>n	land	<u>weed</u>ed
m<u>o</u>m	lĕnd	<u>need</u>ed
n<u>o</u>t	lĕt	<u>nod</u>ded
r<u>o</u>ck	nĕt	<u>rest</u>ed
r<u>o</u>cks	nĕst	<u>twist</u>ed

5. TRICKY WORDS For each word, have students silently figure out the word, then read it aloud.

do   look   one   A   Where

6. DAILY STORY READING

Otters and Seals

Seals are sea mammals   4

too. Seals swim in the sea   10

and rest on the land. See   16

the seals on the rocks.   21

Seals are sleek and   25

swim well. The seals can   30

swim with a whoosh and a   36

swoosh!   37

2

Otters are sea	3
mammals. Otters swim,	6
eat, and rest in the sea.	12
Otters are sleek,	15
smooth, and clean. See	19
them twist in the wet sea.	25
Otters eat clams in the	30
sea. See the otter hit the	36
clam with a rock!	40

1

❶ SOUNDS

Have students say each sound.

❷ WORD DICTATION

Have students count the sounds in each word with their fingers, identify and write each sound, and then read the word. Use the words in sentences as needed.

nest, not, rock, that

The first word is "nest." Tell me the word. (nest)
We're going to count the sounds in "nest."
Tell me the first sound. **Hold up one finger.** (/nnn/)
Repeat with /ĕĕĕ/, /sss/, and /t/.
How many sounds are in "nest"? (Four)

Tell me the first sound. (/nnn/) Write it.
Repeat with /ĕĕĕ/, /sss/, and /t/.
Do Smooth Blending. (/nnnĕĕĕssst/) Read the word. (nest)

Repeat with "not," "rock," and "that."

Note: Tell students to spell the /k/ in "rock" with <u>ck</u>.

CAUTION

Your children may not need Extra Practice. If in doubt, assess students and include Extra Practice only if needed.

HAVE STUDENTS CHECK AND CORRECT.

❸ SENTENCE COMPLETION

Mom sat in the tree.

- Dictate and have students write the first word, "Mom." Remind students to begin the first word of the sentence with a capital letter.
- Have students read and then trace the dotted words to complete the sentence.
- Have students read the sentence.

❹ ACCURACY AND FLUENCY BUILDING

- For each column, have students say any underlined part, then read each word.
- Have students read the whole column.
- Repeat practice on each column, building accuracy first and then fluency.

❺ TRICKY WORDS

Repeat practice, mixing group and individual turns, independent of your voice.

❻ DAILY STORY READING

Proceed to Extra Practice 2 Fluency Passage.

- Have students read each sentence.
- Repeat, mixing group and individual turns, independent of your voice.

❼ EXTRA PRACTICE 2 FLUENCY PASSAGE—CHECKOUT OPPORTUNITY

As you listen to individuals read the story, have students color the picture.

Name_____

1. SOUNDS Have students say each sound.

m	c	oo	ĕ	K	wh	l	o
h	L	ea	n	ar	i	O	t

2. WORD DICTATION Have students count the sounds in each word, identify and write each sound, and then read the word: "nest," "not," "rock," and "that."

1 _____   2 _____   3 _____   4 _____

3. SENTENCE COMPLETION Dictate and have students write "Mom." Have students read and then trace the words to complete the sentence.

_____ sat in the tree.

4. ACCURACY/FLUENCY BUILDING In each column, have students say any underlined part, then read each word. Next, have students read the column.

♥	♥♥	♥♥♥
n<u>o</u>t	clean	on
h<u>o</u>t	clock	Don
sh<u>o</u>t	clam	Dan
d<u>o</u>t	slam	dĕn
l<u>o</u>t	sleek	mĕn

5. TRICKY WORDS For each word, have students silently figure out the word, then read it aloud.

should   is   What   there   wanted

6. DAILY STORY READING

Name_____

FLUENCY PASSAGE

Mom's Room

I went into Mom's room. I needed a   8

rest. I could not rest. There was a little   17

red clock in Mom's room. I had to   25

listen to that clock. Tick tock. Tick tock.   33

Have students read the sentences. Time individual students for 30 seconds; mark errors. To determine words correct per minute (wcpm), count words read in 30 seconds, subtract errors, multiply times two, and record on the chart. If student completes the passage in less than 30 seconds, have him or her return to the top and continue reading. (Repeated readings may be completed with older students, assistants, or parents.)

My goal is to read with 0–2 errors. This is what I did:

Reading	1st	2nd	3rd	4th
Errors				
Words/ 30 seconds				
wcpm				

1 STORYBOOK DECODING REVIEW

For each row, mix group and individual turns, independent of your voice.

2 SOLO STORY REVIEW—UNITS 19 AND 20

- Guide student reading, gradually increasing rate.
- Mix group and individual turns on the stories, independent of your voice.
- Repeat practice. While one student reads, have others track the text with their fingers and whisper read.

3 EXTRA PRACTICE ACTIVITY 3—CHECKOUT OPPORTUNITY

- Have students cut out the Letter Cards and arrange them on the top row of the Letter Card Grid to create the words "on," "not," "hot," "tot," "lot," "lock," "rock," "let," and "net."
- Have students arrange and glue the letters in the remaining rows to create "not, "hot," and "rock."

Challenge Activity: With the remaining letters, have students make a word in the blank row.

1 DECODING PRACTICE 4 REVIEW

For each row, mix group and individual turns, independent of your voice.

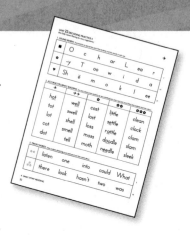

2 SOLO STORY REVIEW—UNITS 21 AND 22

- Guide student reading, gradually increasing rate and emphasizing expression.
- Mix group and individual turns on the stories, independent of your voice.
- Repeat practice. While one student reads, have others track the text with their fingers and whisper read.

3 EXTRA PRACTICE ACTIVITY 4—CHECKOUT OPPORTUNITY

- Have students cut out the Memory Cards. While students are cutting out their cards, listen to individuals read a Solo Story.
- Once the cards have been cut out, have the group or pairs of students play Memory.
  Using one set of cards, spread the cards out in rows with the words facing down.
  Have students take turns. Each time a card is turned over, have the group or pair identify the word.
  If the words match, have students set the pair off to the side.
  If the words do not match, have students turn the cards back over and try again.

o	o	o
t	t	t
e	n	r
h	l	ck

Name_____

Letter Card Grid

	o	t
h		t
r		ck

was	tree	land
was	tree	land
rock	on	the
rock	on	the
Mom	in	in

Note: Memory Cards can also be used to create sentences. Also, please note that there is no match for the word "Mom."